To use
or
not to use?

*Quaker views on
alcohol, drugs and gambling*

Quaker Action on Alcohol and Drugs

ISBN: 0-9553328-0-X (978-0-9553328-0-7)

Published by Quaker Action on Alcohol and Drugs

QAAD
PO Box 2119
Gloucester
GL2 9WW
United Kingdom

Typeset from disk by Compositions by Carn, London N12 8HG

Printed and bound in Great Britain by Ashford Colour Press, Gosport, Hampshire

Dedication

This book is dedicated to the memory of Michael Crewdson and to all those Friends who have sustained and supported QAAD in friendship and in faith.

Foreword

Ben Pink Dandelion

This book is so timely. New legislation on alcohol and gambling, a change in the classification of cannabis, and the ongoing 'success' of the National Lottery, have all faced Friends with a series of challenges and opportunities. What is the corporate Quaker line and what is mine?

The answer to these questions used to be the same for those who had committed themselves to be a part of the Quaker sect. However, in the last 150 years, and particularly in the last fifty, Friends in Britain have increasingly had the ability to interpret their Quakerism individually. After 1860, Friends in Britain could marry non-Quakers without fear of disownment and the practices of 'plain speech' and 'plain dress' became optional and in time anachronistic. The Quaker was invisible and inaudible in the street and, as Elders stopped policing the Quaker home, explicit 'Quaker-time' could be limited to life at the Meeting House. It became up to Friends both to decide what was and what wasn't Quaker in their lifestyle choices, and, how much of their life they wished to share with the rest of Meeting. The twentieth-century shift from a dynastic Quakerism, where most members were born Friends to one where eighty-five per cent joined as adults, led to a weakening of faith transmission as well as a greater ability to attend part-time or as part of a selection of faith affiliations.

British Quakerism, by the twenty-first century then, had become
tolerant and permissive in theological terms but also in terms of
testimony, the witness arising out of the Quaker spiritual
experience. Testimony has changed over time as issues have come
and gone for Friends but more recently, its interpretation has
become individualised. What any part of Quaker testimony
means, whether on peace or integrity or gambling or moderation,
is now up to the individual. In this account, we find Friends
whose behaviour is affirmed by their interpretation of the
testimony whilst others feel a conflict on the very same issues. For
some a conflict is unsettling, for others it isn't. This kind of study
is absolutely crucial if we are to understand the meaning and
content of testimony today. It also reflects on the way we
understand and rationalise testimony or the secular counterpart
of ethics. The authors here cite Jackie Leach Scully's highly
important work on Quaker ethic-building as an act of collage.
Whilst we may tend to measure the moral in terms of
consequences or effects on the people involved, there are no set
principles and no shared moral language, rather we pick and mix
our basis for ethics.

The danger is that 'the tradition' dissolves or becomes an
anachronism that carries authority in the Meeting House but has
little relevance to our everyday life. It may reflect our pious
aspirations but not the comfortable reality of home life. If we do
not drink at the Meeting House but have a glass of wine when we
get home, is the tradition becoming isolated or simply
inappropriate? Or is there a public Quakerism we still wish to
maintain because it stands for a value we still aspire to for society,
a kind of vicarious moral. At Woodbrooke we do not allow alcohol
in public places and do not encourage its consumption. This
doesn't stop people drinking in private but it does signal a value

that alcohol and the kind of work we do neither fit nor need be a part of the social life of the community. It also allows those who eschew alcohol for whatever reason to feel safe and comfortable. The double-life of so many Friends does not then signal a double standard but rather an attempt to live out the duality of a personal and public ethic. But still both are interpreted individually.

Thus, this study gives us a critical insight into what we believe and what we do in the realms of substances and gambling. These are now often invisible behaviours and attitudes and may be part of our lives we construe as unquakerly or decide not to share with our Meetings. Or it may be that we feel we struggle alone with a personal stance unassisted by a Meeting which doesn't seem to want to engage with our lives outside of the Meeting House. This study is crucial for opening up that discussion, for helping all of us both to own our own stances and behaviours and to allow us to think about what a corporate sense of the Meeting might be regarding substances and gambling. It may be we no longer want a corporate line and are happy with the freedoms the present kind of Quakerism gives us but it is surely better that we be explicit about such a change, rather than find ourselves in such a default position.

Key to typefaces:

Text set like this is the main text from QAAD.

Text set in italics is quoted material.

Text set in this typeface indicates a personal story.

CONTENTS

QUAKER ACTION ON ALCOHOL AND DRUGS

This publication has been produced by Quaker Action on Alcohol and Drugs (QAAD). QAAD is a registered charity and a company limited by guarantee. It is managed by a Committee of Quaker Trustees, who between them have a wide range of personal experience and expertise relating to substance use and dependency: their backgrounds include education, medicine, social and legal work and therapy. Trustees are appointed and conduct their business in accordance with Quaker Practice, as observed by the Religious Society of Friends.

QAAD's purpose is to address gambling and the use and misuse of all substances, legal, illegal and prescribed, within a framework of Quaker values. QAAD works mainly within the Religious Society of Friends and offers advice and information, including support and information for Young Friends. When led to do so, we also offer a Quaker perspective on public issues within the realm of our concern.

QAAD has its origins in the Friends Temperance Union, which was founded in 1852 to express a Quaker witness for total abstinence. Moral Welfare was included in the title in the 1960s, when Quakers provided help for families who were under stress

because of alcoholism and assisted those who were trying to
recover from the effects of alcohol. The name was changed again
in the 1990s when the title Quaker Action on Alcohol and Drugs
was adopted. At this time, it was thought that while total
abstinence was still a respected position within the Society of
Friends, it was probably no longer the norm. There were also
increasing concerns about the use and misuse of other substances
and gambling, which all share the possibility of developing into
problematic or addictive behaviours. There are, of course, other
addictive behaviours: while recognising underlying commonalities,
QAAD does not find it possible to encompass them within its
remit.

QAAD is what is known in Quaker circles as a 'listed informal
group'. That is to say, we are recognised by the Religious Society
of Friends as a Quaker body, but we do not speak for Quakers
generally. This book contains the voices of many individual
Quakers, including our own, but it does not reflect an official view
of the Religious Society of Friends (Quakers). Rather, we offer it
as a contribution to the long tradition of Quaker reflection and
action on alcohol, other drugs and gambling.

INTRODUCTION

The beginnings of this book, and the research study on which it is based, date back to 1999, when Quaker Action on Alcohol and Drugs (QAAD) decided to appoint a full-time worker. The decision was taken at that time that the appointee would work mainly within the Religious Society of Friends (Quakers).

At first sight, this might seem odd. Quakers – or Friends as they are also known – have a long-standing testimony against gambling and speculation and one of abstinence or moderation with regard to the use of alcohol and other drugs. However, within wider British society, alcohol, nicotine and – increasingly – illicit drugs, are quite widely available. The National Lottery rapidly gained many 'players', and during the period of the study changes to the gambling laws were initiated. There are also elements of speculation in many aspects of the financial system. Within QAAD we had our own impressions of what the situation might be, but also many questions. How are Quakers responding to these trends in society? What approaches are most helpful for younger Friends? Are Quakers an abstinent or low-consumption group, largely free from problems about use, misuse or dependency? Are these 'out there' concerns, or do they exist for us 'in here'? Above all, we were acutely aware that for many, these are sensitive and painful subjects – and that when the need is greatest, it can be hardest to speak.

QAAD's prime aim is for its work to be relevant to Quakers today. Trustees decided that rather than work from assumption, it would be helpful to gather some information about what Friends' experiences and views actually are – now, at the beginning of the 21st century.

We were very fortunate that Ben Pink Dandelion, tutor in Quaker Studies at the Woodbrooke Study Centre in Birmingham, was prepared to supervise the study. The QAAD appointee, Helena Chambers, undertook the research formally as part of a further degree from Birmingham University. The idea was not just to consider what Friends do, but also how they feel and think on these matters. The inter-relationship between spirituality and Friends' approaches to substances and gambling is, of course, integral.

This book is the result of the study and of deliberations that arose from it. The first chapters have been compiled by QAAD and give some general information about how substance use and gambling have been considered within various religious cultures. This is followed by a brief summary of Quaker history in relation to views on substance use and gambling. The results of the study – in relation to alcohol and other substances, as well as different forms of gambling – are then outlined.

The kernel of the book (in chapters three to seven) is the reflections and personal insights of individual Quakers. These vary from a few words to extended pieces of writing. Some arose from the study itself, while others were commissioned especially for this publication in order to explore particular issues in greater depth. To differentiate these personal voices from the linking text, the shorter ones are printed in italics, while the longer are in a distinctive type-face. These personal contributions are generally anonymous, but when knowledge of the writer's experience or role would assist appreciation or interpretation, some brief information is given. QAAD has provided the linking passages between the quotations and, in parts, relevant quotations from *Quaker Faith and Practice.**

The study suggests that there is a range of experiences amongst Quakers. In the final chapter Helena Chambers considers how we operate as a religious group in relation to substance use and gambling and suggests that some aspects of Quakerism can be particularly inclusive and supportive. At a time when the focus of wider public discussion tends to be mainly drawn to problem behaviours and excess, the book also offers a balanced and perhaps an unusual perspective – by exploring the roots and nature of moderation and abstinence within the Quaker community. This aspect is further explored in the appendix, in which Quaker approaches are related to contemporary perspectives and concerns about gambling, substance use and dependency.

QAAD's aim is to give clear, unbiased information that helps Quakers to make responsible and well-informed choices about substances and gambling within the context of their own circumstances. This book is partly descriptive (in illustrating the experiences of some Quakers) and partly exploratory. We hope that this combination will contribute to Friends' own reflections and we gratefully thank all the Quakers and Quaker Meetings whose experiences and reflections have made it possible.

We must start with a word of apology, or at least of regret, for the rather inelegant and imprecise term 'substances' that is used

---

**Quaker Faith and Practice* is the book of Christian discipline of the Yearly Meeting of the Religious Society of Friends (Quakers) in Britain. All quotations in this volume are taken from the second edition published in 1999.

throughout this book. The word 'drugs' would have been a possibility, but it tends to have associations with illegality – while the phrase 'alcohol, nicotine and other drugs' would have been rather cumbersome. We use the term to cover all the potentially mood-altering chemicals that were included in the study, but not those such as coffee, chocolate or a range of medical and illicit substances that were beyond the scope of the research project.

Helena Chambers, (Director of QAAD),
Eva Deregowska (Trustee of QAAD),
Sandra Hobbs (Clerk of QAAD) and
Graham Thomas (Assistant Clerk of QAAD)
May, 2006.

CHAPTER 1
HISTORICAL CONTEXT

1. General religious attitudes to gambling and the use of substances

Within many religious traditions, gambling and the use of drugs have been seen as having powerful spiritual and ethical dimensions. In the case of substance use, the capacity of drugs to alter the state of consciousness has been particularly important in a religious context. Within some religions, this quality has lead to caution about use or to advice about abstinence. In others, drugs have been used in a controlled way in religious ritual or to enhance visionary experience (for example, the use of the peyote cactus root in some North American Indian tribes[1]). Religious attitudes may vary with the substance: for example, a cannabis infusion was used as an enhancement to spiritual practices by Brahmins within the Hindu tradition, but alcohol use was avoided.[2] In Western Christianity and Judaism, where alcohol was the main substance available, its use in religious practice tends to be sacramental and symbolic – most obviously in the Catholic mass.

---

[1] Described in *The Doors of Perception* Huxley, A. Chatto & Windus Ltd 1954
[2] Carstairs, G. (1958) Daru and Bhang: Cultural Factors in the Choice of Intoxicant, *Quarterly Journal in the Studies of Alcohol* 15, 220-237 (cited in J. Orford, 1995 *Excessive Appetites* p 158)

*The urge to transcend self-conscious selfhood is, as I have
said, a principal appetite of the soul. When, for whatever
reason, men and women fail to transcend themselves by
means of worship, good works and spiritual exercises,
they are apt to resort to religion's chemical surrogates...*

The Doors of Perception,
Aldous Huxley, 1954

Gambling, too, has been considered in a variety of ways within
religious and spiritual traditions. Within some, appealing to
chance has been seen as a way in which the will of God or gods
can be expressed. In others (including the Protestant tradition,
for example) appealing to chance rather than relying on God has
been seen as sinful.

Another relevant factor is the strand of asceticism in both
Eastern and Western traditions. This involves restraint from
sensual gratification and, in many religions, the avoidance of
mood-altering drugs. The origin of the word asceticism implies a
training of the self (from the Greek 'askeein', meaning to work,
exercise or train). From this outlook, it is undesirable to take a
substance that intoxicates, or that changes the functioning of the
senses or emotions – or does so in a way that encourages sensual
appetites, materialism or a focus on worldly pleasures. These
preoccupations are seen as distractions from God or spirit.

*God gave us our faculties to work with, and everything
will have its due reward; there is no reason, then, for
trying to cast a spell over them – they must be allowed to
perform their office until God gives them a better one.*

St Teresa of Avila 'Interior Castle' (1588)

From an ascetic perspective, gambling is also a worldly and
materialistic activity likely to hinder spiritual progress. This

strand of thinking is expressed in some early Christian traditions[3] and was a particular influence on Protestantism.

If you call yourself a Christian when you are a dice-player, you say you are what you are not, for you are a partner with the world.

Tertullian, Christian writer, AD 160 – 220

An ascetic perspective tends to view gambling or substance use as damaging in itself and therefore not to be undertaken at all. Within a Christian context, this perspective could become woven into the concept of sin – that is, that certain actions or motives are inherently harmful and are offences against God. Within some Protestant denominations, gambling and drinking (or drunkenness) were considered sinful in this way.

Other objections have been rooted in ethical concerns about the consequences to either the individual or to others of gambling or substance use. This focus means that if the bad consequences can be avoided, the activity itself may sometimes be acceptable. In this way, Thomas Aquinas[4] felt that gambling could be permitted if it were not motivated by covetousness, unfairly undertaken (with loaded dice) or if it did not exploit the young and psychologically immature. As regards alcohol, a stress on the consequences of drunkenness (rather than on the drinking of alcohol *per se*) can lead towards adopting moderation rather than abstinence.

---

[3] The Roman centurions playing dice for Jesus' cloak at the crucifixion in an obvious example of gambling as profane behaviour.

[4] Quoted in D H Field, 'Gambling' in D J Atkinson & D H Field (eds) *New Dictionary of Christian Ethics and Pastoral Theology* (Leicester, IVP, 1995) p 402. Thomas Aquinas, *Summa Theologiae*, Vols 34 & 40, Eyre & Spottiswoode, 1972

What is life to one who is without wine? It has been
created to make people happy. Wine drunk at the proper
time and in moderation is rejoicing of heart and gladness
of soul. Wine drunk to excess leads to bitterness of spirit,
to quarrels and stumbling. Drunkenness increases the
anger of a fool to his own hurt, reducing his strength and
adding wounds.

(Ecclesiasticus 31: 25-30)

Addiction is one obvious potential ill-effect of both substance use
and gambling. Addiction as we understand it now is actually a
relatively modern concept, which has been developed during the
past two centuries: it differentiates behaviour that is dependent
from that which may be excessive, unsafe or related to the harms
caused by intoxication. However, the social, family and personal
consequences of all such behaviours had long been the subject of
religious concern. Within the Christian tradition, this included the
perspective of St Paul, that one's own behaviour, even if not
harmful, may encourage what we would now term 'misuse' in
others.

It is good not to eat meat or drink wine or do anything
that makes your brother or sister stumble.

(1 Romans 14: 21)

Again, this early stress on the importance of example continued
within the Christian tradition – particularly in Protestant
thinking – as one of the motivations for abstinence or restrained
behaviour for both drinking and gambling.

Within some religious groups, some or all of these concerns have
led to precepts that order or advise abstinence. For other groups,
the standard is of moderation, with the aim of preventing excess
– or there may be conditions or parameters specified that would

assist ethical behaviour. There are also some religious groups that do not take a particular stance on either substance use or gambling.

St Benedict's Rule
Chapter 40. The proper amount of drink

Everyone has his own gift from God, one this and another that (1 Cor. 7:7). It is, therefore, with some uneasiness that we specify the amount of food and drink for others. However, with due regard for the infirmities of the sick, we believe that a half bottle of wine a day is sufficient for each. But those to whom God gives the strength to abstain must know that they will earn their own reward.

The superior will determine when local conditions, work or the summer heat indicates the need for a greater amount. He must, in any case, take great care lest excess or drunkenness creep in. We read that monks should not drink wine at all, but since the monks of our day cannot be convinced of this, let us at least agree to drink moderately, and not to the point of excess, for wine makes even wise men go astray. However, where local circumstances dictate an amount much less than what is stipulated above, or even none at all, those who live there should bless God and not grumble. Above all else we admonish them to refrain from grumbling.

2. Does religious affiliation affect gambling and substance use?

During the latter half of the twentieth century, interest began to
grow into the question of whether religious adherence might
actually have an influence on substance use or gambling –
particularly in the behaviour of the young. Studies were
undertaken, and showed that there is indeed a relationship, at
least for some groups. The evidence suggests – perhaps not
surprisingly – that the stance taken by the religious group is
important: when a religious group strongly forbids drinking, other
drug use or gambling, members of the group are less likely to
undertake these activities.

In Britain and North America, studies have compared the
behaviour of people in various (mainly Christian) denominations.
Protestants tend to show lower rates of substance use and misuse
than do Catholics. Protestant groups that strongly forbid these
behaviours (for example, Mormons or Latter Day Saints) show
lower rates than 'Liberal' Protestant groups,[5] which do not enjoin
abstinence but advise moderation or the avoidance of excess. The
findings about gambling have been fewer, but have reached
broadly similar conclusions. Some studies of young people have
also suggested that those who depart from the denomination's
approach to alcohol are more likely to smoke nicotine, try illicit
substances and – in some cases – to gamble.

---

[5] Hanson, D.J. (1974) Drinking attitudes and behaviour among college
students. *Journal of Alcohol and Drug Education* 19, 6-14; Bock, W. E., and
Cochran J. (1987) Moral Messages: The relative influence of denomination on
the religiosity – alcohol relationship. *The Sociological Quarterly* 28,1: 89 – 103;
Burkett, S.R. and White, M. (1974) Hellfire and Delinquency: Another Look.
Journal for the Scientific Study of Religion 13:455-462; Perkins H.W. (1985)
Religious traditions, parents, and peers as determinants of alcohol and drug
use among college students. *Review of Religious Research* 27 : 15-31.

What reasons have been suggested for this link?

The most well established explanation is that the strength of the religious prohibition against substance use or gambling is the critical factor. An early idea was that the prospect of punishment in the afterlife might be an influence on religious people – a theory that rejoiced in the title of the 'hellfire hypothesis'.[6] Later explanations concentrated more on the psychological processes through which a strong religious standard becomes 'internalised' in the individual – for children and the young, this would be through a combination of religious texts and precepts, the authority of clergy or religious leaders, religious education and parental influence. Later, contact between members of the group would lead to more reinforcement. The suggestion is that those who act outside their religious precepts on substance use and gambling are likely to feel psychological discomfort (that is, 'cognitive dissonance'), or else to become subject to social pressures from within their group. These influences would tend to encourage them to return to the accepted religious norm. It has also been suggested that the same processes could work in the opposite direction, and that those who depart from religious precepts in one way may be inclined to do so in another. They would then be subject to mounting disapproval and become progressively more disengaged.

This kind of explanation for low rates of substance use and gambling in religious people has focused on 'conditioning' processes. Another approach has been to focus on spirituality, though relatively little formal research has been conducted on this. The fact that some methods of tackling addiction include a

[6] Hirschi, T. and Stark, R. (1969) Hellfire and Delinquency. *Social Problems* 17:202-213

spiritual dimension (most notably the Twelve steps of Alcoholics Anonymous) has added credence to this proposal. Interest is growing in the role of spiritual life in both use and dependency.[7]

Another explanation has been that ascetic attitudes discourage substance use and gambling and some studies have given support to this proposition. A linked idea is that the moral outlook of those with patterns of abstinence or low consumption may be influential. A British study among students[8] found that they were less likely to engage in substance use or misuse if they held the belief that this kind of behaviour is a sign of moral weakness in a person – and also if they thought that members of their own denomination would be unlikely to behave in such a way.

There has been some debate about the relationship between religious groups and levels of problems or dependency, because on this question there has been a mixture of evidence. Much of it shows lower rates of use and problem behaviours in groups with strong prohibitions against substance use or gambling. This suggests such an approach may have preventative effects.

However, a few studies also showed that when people from the 'prohibiting' religious groups do drink alcohol, higher rates of problems were found.[9] One explanation for this was that such people may not have learned a 'healthy' pattern of control for

---

[7] See, for example, Miller, W.R. (1998). Researching the spiritual dimensions of alcohol and other drug problems. *Addiction* 93(7) 979-990.
[8] Jolly S, Orford J. (1983). Religious observance, attitudes towards drinking, and knowledge about drinking, amongst university students. *Alcohol and Alcoholism*.Vol.18 No.3 pp. 271-278.
[9] Skolnick, Jerome. (1958) 'Religious Affiliation and Drinking Behavior', *Quarterly Journal for Studies on Alcohol*, 19: 452-470; Mizruchi, Ephraim H. and Perrucci, Robert. (1962) 'Norm qualities and differential effects of deviant behavior: An exploratory analysis.' *American Sociological Review*, 27, 391-399; Schlegel R.P., Sanborn MD. (1979)

drinking. Others think that substance misuse and gambling are ways of showing rebellion or disengagement, particularly in young people. A further suggestion is that when people develop problems with substances or gambling, they are deviating from both social and religious norms, and standards of many kinds may have less impact on the individual. Finally, the idea has been advanced that when people from a strict religious group begin to drink, or to drink problematically, they find the inconsistency (or cognitive dissonance) too painful and tend to leave their denomination.[10] In this analysis, groups like Catholics that do not have strong advice against alcohol use might retain such adherents within the religious fold, when other groups tend to lose them.

These studies have many implications for faith groups, particularly with regard to the education of children and in relation to preventing problems and supporting people through them. One reading of the evidence suggests that the strong assertion of an abstinence principle or one of low use is likely to result in fewer problems of misuse or dependency. Another suggests that this may be the outcome for the majority, but that those who depart from the religious standard or go on to develop problems may do so at a higher level, or may risk going unsupported.

When this study began, it was not known whether the results would illuminate these questions, but this background was a helpful starting point. The other was Quaker history and its influence on our attitudes today.

---

[10] Mullen, K, Williams, R, and Hunt, K. (1996) Irish descent, religion, and alcohol and tobacco use. *Addiction*, 91,2, 243-254.

3. Attitudes to gambling and substance use in Quaker history

Early Quaker history

The origins of Quakerism are in seventeenth century Protestantism, and Quakers shared the abstemious attitude of other Protestant groups towards gambling and the drinking of alcohol. Though Quaker attitudes were part of this general movement, George Fox's journal also illustrates several specific strands of thinking, which can be traced through Quaker history and into the present day.

An early entry in George Fox's journal reads:

> *When I came towards nineteen years of age, I being upon business at a fair, one of my cousins, whose name was Bradford, being a professor* and having another professor with him, came to me and asked me to drink part of a jug of beer with them, and I, being thirsty, went in with them, for I loved any that had a sense of good, or did seek after the Lord. And when we had drunk a glass apiece, they began to drink healths and called for more drink, agreeing together that he that would not drink should pay all. I was grieved that any that made profession of religion should offer to do so. They grieved me very much, having never had such a thing put to me before by any sort of people; wherefore I rose up to be gone, and putting my hand into my pocket, I took out a groat and laid it down upon the table before them and said, 'If it be so, I'll leave you'. So I went away; and when I had done business I had to do, I returned home...'*

> * that is, one who professes religion

> Extract from George Fox's *Journal*, 1643
> (quoted in *Quaker Faith and Practice* 19.01) [11]

At the time when George Fox was living and writing, the water supply was uncertain and 'small beer' was the safer and normal alternative. He drank to quench thirst, but avoided immoderation or excess, finding it contrary to religious 'profession'. His way of making his stance plain was personal action (rather than by expressing disapproval, it seems).

A concern about tobacco and its congruity with religious 'profession' is also apparent in an early minute from Hardshaw Monthly Meeting (tobacco being the other substance commonly available at this period). Again, the avoidance of excess is stressed, but also the importance of not undertaking such behaviour in public – perhaps because of the power of example.

> *It being discoursed that the common excess of smoking tobacco is inconsistent with our holy profession, this Meeting adviseth that such as have occasion to make use of it do take it privately, neither in their labour nor employment, nor by the highways, nor in alehouses, nor elsewhere too publicly.*
>
> Hardshaw Monthly Meeting, 1691
> (quoted in *Quaker Faith and Practice* 20.37)

Although the concept of addiction was yet to be construed in the way that we now understand it, George Fox's stress on the spiritual aspects of addiction foreshadows some later approaches to the subject, which stress the common psychological and spiritual elements that are involved across the range of addictions. He did not focus specifically on substances or on

---

[11] *Quaker Faith and Practice* is the book of Christian discipline of the Yearly Meeting of the Religious Society of Friends (Quakers) in Britain. It describes the organisation and practices of the Quaker community, and the values that underlie them. It also contains Quaker writings from over the centuries that assist worship and spiritual reflection, and give advice for daily living.

gambling, but addresses the subject more generally in terms of
any preoccupation that can gain ascendancy over the spirit:

> *Friends, whatever ye are addicted to, the tempter will come
> in that thing: and when he can trouble you, then he gets
> advantage over you, and then you are gone. Stand still in
> that which is pure, and after ye see yourselves, and then
> mercy comes in. After thou seest thy thoughts, and thy
> temptations, do not think, but submit; and then power
> comes. Stand still in that which shows and discovers; and
> then doth strength immediately come. And stand still in
> the Light, and submit to it, and the other will be hushed
> and gone; and then content comes.*
>
> George Fox, 1652, quoted in
> *Quaker Faith and Practice* 20.42.

George Fox's careful attitude to alcohol was continued in
eighteenth century Quakerism. However, abstinence was still not
the expectation – rather the avoidance of excess or the
'appearance of evil':

> *As temperance and moderation are virtues proceeding
> from true religion…we beseech all to be careful of their
> conduct and behaviour, abstaining from every appearance
> of evil; and excess in drinking has been too prevalent
> among many of the inhabitants of these nations, we
> commend to all Friends a watchful care over themselves,
> attended with a religious and prudent zeal against a
> practice so dishonourable and pernicious.*
>
> Yearly Meeting in London, 1751
> (quoted in *Quaker Faith and Practice*, 20.38)

The emergence of Temperance

The unsafe water supply and the perception of excess as the problem (rather than the use of alcohol *per se*) meant that some Quakers were involved in the brewing industry during the earlier history of Quakerism. However, the late eighteenth and early nineteenth centuries saw the beginnings of profound social concern about the detrimental effects of alcohol. The availability of cheap, potent alcohol (particularly gin) amongst the urbanised poor and 'free trade' measures that opened up the market exacerbated poverty, disorder and ill-health at a time when a disciplined workforce was required for emerging industrial processes. Hogarth's *Gin Lane* captures the early phase of this concern.

In the wake of such problems, the Temperance Movement developed during the course of the nineteenth century. Initially, the term was used in the literal sense of moderation, but later total abstinence became more widespread an interpretation and 'temperance' came to be associated with desisting from alcohol entirely. Much Temperance membership was drawn from non-Conformist Protestant sects, and Quakers constituted a leading part of this movement. Quaker Action on Alcohol and Drugs has its origins in the Friends Temperance Union (FTU), which was formed in 1852.

The formation of the FTU was preceded by a lively and protracted debate about temperance in the columns of *The British Friend*. Some correspondents urged the positives of total abstinence as setting a good example to others. The discussion was conducted mainly in a Biblical framework, often with particular reference to the writings of St Paul. One such correspondent concluded:

> *'moderation' is, in my opinion, not in accordance with*
> *the principles and tenets of Holy Scripture.*
>
> Letter to *The British Friend*,[12] Fourthmonth, 1851

Others noted that Jesus was not himself abstinent and focused on the wisdom of trusting the relationship of each individual with God and with their conscience.

> *The only means that are, or can be, legitimately*
> *employed, are those of information as to the facts,*
> *arguments respecting their consequences, and persuasion*
> *as to the example recommended. With this view...the*
> *consciences of the individual may safely be left to lead*
> *them to their own conclusions, under that promised*
> *guidance of the Holy Spirit which is the experience of all*
> *those who seek it...*
>
> Letter to *The British Friend*, Thirdmonth, 1851

The latter strain of thought led another correspondent to argue against the Society of Friends using any of its formal means to advance abstinence amongst Friends:

> *the adoption of it (abstinence) as a rule, or even as a*
> *strong advice, is far from being desirable...it should*
> *derive from personal conviction...*
>
> Letter to *The British Friend*, Fourthmonth, 1851

This desire not to judge others is often illustrated in the correspondence and is apparent in Temperance supporters as well

---

[12] *The British Friend* is the predecessor of the current periodical *The Friend*. It is the Quaker weekly journal that has offered independent Quaker journalism since its inception in 1843. In the nineteenth century, Quakers did not use named months, but referred to them in terms of numbers.

as in those who inclined towards moderation. One Temperance
advocate put it thus:

> *We are not left at liberty harshly to judge, or*
> *unceremoniously to condemn, those who from whatever*
> *motive, persist in strict moderation.*
>
> Letter to *The British Friend*, Fourthmonth, 1851.

Abstinence seems to have gained considerable ground amongst
Friends during the latter half of the nineteenth century. The FTU
records note, for example, that prior to the visit of one of their
speakers to Birmingham, seventy to eighty Friends in the area
covered by the Meeting were abstainers. Afterwards, 130 out of
the 300 members of the Meeting declared themselves so. Work
with children was also undertaken through the Band of Hope,
which involved pledges to abstinence. Another telling indication
of the prevalence of Temperance thinking amongst Quakers is
found in the general withdrawal from involvement in the brewing
industry.

The influence of the Temperance movement within Quakerism is
likely to have been enhanced by the effective public role its
members played in influencing wider social policy and legislation.
The work of Joseph Rowntree was pioneering in its sociological
investigation into whether the deprivation of the poor was
increased by the consumption of alcohol. He concluded that this
was the case for some, and Quakers also played a prominent part
in pressure to reform licensing laws at the end of the nineteenth
century.[13]

During the latter part of the century, members of the Rowntree
family and other Quakers were active in the campaign against the

---

[13] Rowntree, J. and Shadwell, R. (1899) *The Temperance Problem and Social Reform*

opium trade and pointed up concerns about the role of opium
amongst the rural and urban poor of England. Joshua Rowntree
also collated evidence for a Parliamentary Commission on the
impact of opium production on the rural people of India.[14]

During the nineteenth century, Quakerism tended to be identified
with temperance at both a public and private level. While
decisions about abstinence remained a matter of personal
conscience, this general pattern persisted well into the twentieth
century.

Throughout this time, a concern about the spiritual impact of
alcohol use continued to be apparent – particularly in relation to
young people. The FTU combined with Central Education
Committee to produce leaflets and information for them, in which
this is discussed:

> *We have no wish merely to impose our views on the*
> *children but to offer them the material to help them to*
> *ascertain for themselves that the development of man's*
> *spiritual powers is more possible in an alcohol-free body*
> *than in others.*
>
> Central Education Committee, 1935
> (FTU records, lodged at Friends House Library)

---

[14] He wrote, for example, 'It does not seem to have occurred to the Government
that any representation of the peasants was needful. The statements of
landowners and managers were deemed sufficient...'

20th century developments

In the middle of the twentieth century, indications emerge that the subject of abstinence once more becomes a source of debate among Friends. L. Hugh Doncaster drew attention to the matter:

> *My intention is not to divide Friends, but to raise for frank discussion and clarification a question which is too often sidestepped, and which should no longer be brushed aside. I am concerned to examine two main questions: the first is, Have Friends had a testimony concerning intoxicants, and if so, what was it and has it been given up? The second... What is our responsibility in this matter now, and how can it find expression, and be strengthened by, the corporate witness of the Society of Friends?'*
>
> Friends Testimony on Intoxicants, 1954

However, his conviction of abstinence as a Quaker testimony is not placed in opposition to individual judgement in these matters:

> *...right habits of living should grow from deep inner conviction, and not be imposed as rules or regulations...*

As the latter half of the twentieth century progressed, Friends seemed increasingly to tend towards moderation. Towards the end of the century, this is reflected in the wording on the web-site of Britain Yearly Meeting:

> *One testimony that Quakers have had to give careful thought to is our testimony on moderation. In the nineteenth century Quakers saw the bad effects that drink and drunkenness had in society. Along with other Nonconformist Christians they campaigned against alcohol. Many Quakers were active in the Temperance Movement*

*– a movement of people who 'took the pledge' (promising
that they would never drink alcohol) as a witness against
the evils it caused.*

*Nowadays, we emphasize the need for moderation, though
some still take a stand against all alcohol.*[15]

This approach was reflected in the broadening of QAAD's own
position during the 1990s, to include both moderation and
abstinence.

During the latter part of the twentieth century, the availability of
illicit drugs presented Quakers with challenges, along with the
rest of society. As the century moved to its close, further
information about the risks of drug use – including tobacco – also
had an influence on Quaker attitudes and behaviour. A practical
manifestation of this was the development of guidelines by the
Children and Young People's Section at Friends House, which
mounts and supports residential events for young people. The
guidelines work to prevent the use of illicit drugs and to manage
and minimise alcohol and tobacco use.

However, while some frames of reference (legal or medical) focus
on the properties or status of particular substances, from the time
of George Fox's insight into addiction, Quakers have often
stressed the commonalities between different kinds of drug use.
This approach concentrates on the underlying spiritual, emotional
and social dimensions of substance use and misuse, in relation to
both cause and effect. These insights provide the core of the
guidance in the current edition of *Quaker Faith and Practice*.

*In view of the harm done by the use of alcohol, tobacco
and other habit-forming drugs, consider whether you*

---

[15] BYM website: *http://www.quaker.org.uk*

*should limit your use of them or refrain from using them
altogether. Remember that any use of alcohol or drugs
may impair judgement and put both the user and others
in danger.*

Quaker Faith and Practice,
Advices and Queries 1.02.40

*Many yearly meetings hold very strong testimonies
against any use of tobacco or alcohol. Within Britain
Yearly Meeting some Friends advocate total abstinence
from alcohol, others counsel moderation. Those who smoke
tobacco, drink alcohol, or abuse other substances risk
damage to their own health, and may hurt or endanger
other people. Such use can deaden a person's sensitivity
and response to others and to God. Consider whether you
should avoid these products altogether, discourage their use
in others, especially young people, and refrain from any
share in their manufacture or sale. Maintain your own
integrity and do not let social pressures influence your
decisions.*

1994, Quaker Faith and Practice, 20.40

Another passage in the current edition of *Quaker Faith and
Practice* combines a Quaker perspective on addiction with a
modern psychological approach to the underlying connections
between different kinds of dependency:

*For those trapped in substance abuse, such advice (as in
20.40) may seem hollow. Commonalities exist between
addictive behaviours with these substances and other
compulsive actions such as in the areas of eating
disorders, gambling, overwork and physical abuse. The
causes go deep and may not be fully understood, but the
resulting pain, fear, desperation and denial, damaging*

*the abuser and all around that person, need to be
supportively recognised. A Meeting community should be
ready to listen non-judgementally, offer information about
sources of help, refuse to enable people to continue in
harmful patterns, and continue to offer an environment
free from addictive practices.*
                    Faith and practice, Baltimore Yearly Meeting, 1988
                    (quoted in *Quaker Faith and Practice*, 20.41)

One reading of Quaker history – at least in relation to alcohol –
would suggest a trend from moderation towards abstinence, and
later back towards moderation. However, beneath these
transitions, certain values and strands of thinking have remained
constant, and form the warp and weft of the Quaker picture.
These abiding preoccupations concern the relationship between
religious conviction and substance use; the effect of substances on
the spirit; the role of example and the effect of one's behaviour
on others; the need for personal conduct to be based on
conviction; and a stress on the links between different kinds of
dependency.

Attitudes to gambling in Quaker history

Quaker attitudes to gambling have some common roots with
attitudes to alcohol:

*Are friends careful to avoid all vain sports, places of
diversion, gaming, and all unnecessary frequenting of
alehouses or taverns, excess in drinking, and
intemperance of every kind?*
                    London Yearly Meeting Discipline 1755
                    (extracts from Minutes and Advices, page 196)

Friends also held the perspective that gambling fosters the belief
that material things are the source of satisfaction, and encourages

greed and envy. At the time when speculation as we understand it began to arise in a modern economy, Friends took an early and strong stance in seeing it as a form of gambling:

> *This Meeting has been deeply affected with the reproach brought on truth and Friends, by the misconduct of some under our name, who through an evil covetousness, have engaged dealings in the public stocks, or government securities; which is a species of gaming, and altogether inconsistent with our religious principles.*
>
> London Yearly Meeting Discipline, 1788.

The allying of any irresponsible or greedy use of money (even through formal or 'respectable' channels) with gambling remains a strong strand in Quaker thinking. The Quaker approach to gambling is also rooted in the testimonies to integrity and honesty. Possessions and money are a trust, and must be handled in a spirit of stewardship. Profits should be proportionate to effort and not gained at the expense of others:

> *Gambling disregards our belief that possessions are a trust. The persistent appeal to covetousness evident, for example, in football pool propaganda is fundamentally opposed to the unselfishness which was taught by Jesus Christ and by the New Testament as a whole...*
>
> Quaker Faith and Practice, 1959 (and 1994: 20.61)

These strands are further explored in other passages in *Quaker Faith and Practice* (1994):

> *Consider which of the ways to happiness offered by society are truly fulfilling and which are potentially corrupting and destructive. Be discriminating when choosing means of entertainment and information. Resist*

*the desire to acquire possessions or income through
unethical investment, speculation, or games of chance.*

Advices and Queries in *Quaker Faith and Practice*, 1.02

The advent of the National Lottery in 1994 also brought these
issues into focus. After a full consultation process with Friends
and Meetings, a public statement was issued by the Clerk of
Meeting for Sufferings[16] in November 1995, which re-asserted
many of Friends' traditional concerns about gambling:

> *The Religious Society of Friends in Britain has today
> strongly confirmed their 350 year stand against games of
> chance and adopted this statement on the National
> Lottery and Public Life... Quakers are totally opposed to
> the promotion of large-scale lottery by government...*
> * *It fosters the attitude that it is right to hope for
>   something for nothing*
> * *It is a misuse of resources when many basic human
>   needs are not fully met*
> * *It promotes an addiction to gambling, exacerbated by
>   the addition of Instant Game scratch-cards to the
>   scheme*
> * *It increases the gross inequality between the majority of
>   people and a small number of millionaires*
> * *It encourages the belief that fulfilment and happiness
>   depend upon riches*

---

[16] Meeting for Sufferings is a body that was founded in 1675, originally to
redress or record the sufferings of Quakers who could be imprisoned or suffer in
other ways for their religious convictions. The functions of Meeting for
Sufferings evolved, and it now acts as 'a central body which can act on behalf
of the Society [of Friends] between Yearly Meetings.' (*Quaker Faith and
Practice*, 7.01). Yearly Meeting is an annual gathering for all members of the
Religious Society of Friends, at which religious matters are discussed, and
decisions are taken.

A further public statement re-stating the Quaker position was issued in December, 1996, and the Society of Friends divested itself of financial holdings in any companies associated with the Lottery.

On the tenth anniversary of the Lottery, in September 2004, Meeting for Sufferings issued a further statement re-affirming its position and addressing current concerns about the uses of National Lottery funding. It reiterated the fundamental grounds of objection and added:

> *The National Lottery offends our belief about loving our neighbours and sharing resources. We wish to stand together, as members of Churches Together in Britain & Ireland (CTBI) and with all who share our values, against the rush to become a gambling society...*
>
> *We are disturbed by the accelerating substitution of National Lottery funds for planned public funding of social projects. Quakers will continue to press the government to fulfil its responsibilities for social and economic welfare through normal public institutions. We are totally opposed to the promotion of a large-scale lottery by government and wish to see the National Lottery ended.*

Many Friends have voluntary or professional involvement with charities or voluntary agencies that might benefit from National Lottery funding. The issues and dilemmas this raises for Friends were considered in a consultation process and published in a book called *Role Over* in 2004. This concluded that Friends had a shared feeling of concern about state-sponsored gambling and a strong feeling that 'public and charitable projects should not be dependent upon it.'

Objections to gambling and relying on the role of chance have
also meant that Quakers traditionally avoided small-scale raffles –
including those for charitable purposes.

The traditional Quaker witness against gambling has continued
into its various manifestations in modern life, and is set out on
the website of Britain Yearly Meeting:[17]

> *Nor would we consider that money 'made' by playing the*
> *stock market was truly earned. Because we believe we*
> *should not profit from other people's loss, we do not*
> *gamble in any way so you will not find Quakers betting*
> *on horses, buying National Lottery tickets or organising*
> *raffles (preferring in the last two cases to give money*
> *directly to charity).*

The website also summarises some of the connections between the
values that underlie Quaker attitudes to substance use and
gambling:

> *In the nineteenth century this social awareness showed*
> *itself in the campaigns against alcohol as Friends saw*
> *the dire consequences of drink and drunkenness. Friends*
> *today emphasise the need for moderation, though some*
> *still take a stand against alcohol. It was a similar*
> *sensitivity to social ills that resulted in an opposition to*
> *gambling where a few win at the expense of many.*

Summary

The Quaker position on gambling has continued more or less
unchanged and essentially involves a stance of abstinence. That
on substance use has seen more development, but is essentially
one of 'moderation and abstinence,' as described in *Quaker Faith
and Practice*. The Puritan heritage could tend towards an ascetic

---

[17] *www.quaker.org.uk*

outlook – but there is also a Quaker tradition of liberality in matters of personal belief and conviction. For contemporary Quakers, the other relevant legacy of Quakerism is the prime importance of spiritual experience. All of these aspects were considered in the study, but Friends who participated were also given space to put forward other elements that were important to them in considering these subjects.

CHAPTER 2
THE QUAKER STUDY

1. Introduction

The Quaker study surveyed 159 Friends from five Preparative Meetings[18] across England, Wales and Scotland and from Young Friends General Meeting (YFGM).[19] Within Preparative Meetings, all who attended Meeting for Worship on a particular Sunday were asked to participate: no selection was made. Similarly, at YFGM all who attended a residential weekend gathering were asked to participate. Nearly seventy per cent of those asked responded to the survey.

Participants were asked about their past and their present behaviour with regard to a large range of licit and illicit substances. The substances were: alcohol; nicotine; cannabis; stimulant drugs (ecstasy, amphetamines and cocaine); hallucinogenic drugs (LSD and magic mushrooms); and opiates (heroin and methadone). As regards gambling, the survey also asked about raffles, the National Lottery and various other forms of betting such as casino betting

---

[18] Preparative Meetings are established Meetings for Worship for Quakers at the local level. They have a variety of functions, including regular Meetings for Church Affairs. (*Quaker Faith and Practice* 4.28- 32, and 4.37- 4.39)

[19] Young Friends General Meeting is the body for young Friends between the ages of 18 and 30ish. It holds four or five large gatherings every year, as well as local events. The survey was undertaken at one of the regular national Meetings.

and horse racing. Friends who participated were also asked about their reasons for their behaviour.

In statistical terms, 159 people is a small 'sample' so it is not possible to say that it represents Quakers generally. Although the response rate was good by normal statistical standards, some Friends chose not to participate, which also limits the 'generalisability' of the study. The study can, however, be viewed as a snapshot of a reasonable number of Quaker members and attenders at a range of Meetings on a particular day.

Care must also be taken in drawing comparisons with figures derived from far larger surveys of the population at large in Britain. However, occasionally some rough comparisons are made to give context – and we begin with some general information about substance use and gambling in society generally.

2. Substance use: what are the general patterns in society?

In society generally, alcohol is a legal substance and the most widely used, with approximately ninety per cent of the population taking it on at least some occasions. There are, however, some relevant patterns of distribution that involve both drinking and problem drinking.

People in more advantaged social and economic classes tend to drink more regularly and are less likely to be abstinent or to drink less than one unit per week. Men (but not women) from less privileged classes are slightly more likely to drink at very high or hazardous levels. Men are also more likely to exceed weekly limits, with about twelve per cent of men and six per cent of women drinking in this way.[20]

---

[20] Office of National Statistics figures quoted by Alcohol Concern (www.alcoholconcern.org.uk)

Both regularity and amount of drinking have traditionally tended
to be lesser amongst women: whilst this is still the case, the signs
are that the pattern is equalising and some of the strongest
concerns have been expressed about the rise in the drinking
pattern of young women. One of the reasons for concern is that
physical damage from the excessive use of alcohol tends to
happen more quickly and more seriously to women than to men.

DEPARTMENT OF HEALTH GUIDELINES

Per day
Up to 4 units of alcohol per day for men
Up to 3 units of alcohol per day for women
**Consumption of 4-8 units for men and 3-6 for women carries
some health risk**
Consumption in excess of this is classed as heavy drinking

Per week
Low consumption is classed as 1-10 units per week for men,
1-7 for women
Moderate consumption 10-21 units per week for men, 7-14
for women
High consumption 22-35 units for men,
15-21 for women
Very high consumption 36-50 units for men,
22-40 for women

Consumptions in excess of this are classed as hazardous

**A UNIT OF ALCOHOL IS USUALLY DEFINED AS HALF A
PINT OF NORMAL STRENGTH BEER, A SMALL GLASS
OF WINE (125 ml), OR A SMALL SHERRY OR WHISKY**

Much attention has been given to 'risky single occasion drinking' (so called 'binge drinking') in recent years, which is defined as drinking twice the daily recommended limit (so eight units for men and six units for women are categorised as binge drinking). This tends to occur at higher rates in young people under twenty-four, with over a third of men and a quarter of young women having done so in the last week.[21] However, the pattern persists into middle age with about a third of men and a fifth of women reporting doing so in the last week.[22]

Nicotine tends to be used more by people in the least advantaged social groups, and least by those with the highest social and economic status. Rates of smoking are also highest among young people. Boys and men used to smoke more, but now the gender balance is roughly equal. Just over a quarter of the adult population smoke.

As regards illicit substances, there are several patterns of variation within the larger statistics that are available through surveys and studies. It remains true that use of these substances occurs mainly amongst young people – though not exclusively so. Men tend to use these substances at higher rates than women – experimentally, regularly and problematically.[23] Social and economic circumstances and level of education also have an influence. The use of some illicit substances (particularly cocaine) tend to show a 'U' shaped curve, whereby the highest levels of drug use tend to be at the two extremes of the household income scales, while the lowest prevalence is in the middle-income groups.'[24] A similar 'U' shaped pattern tends to be found in

---

[21 & 22] Office of National Statistics figures quoted by Alcohol Concern (www.alcoholconcern.org.uk)
[23 & 24] Ramsey, M and Partridge, C. Drug Misuse Declared in 1998: results from the British Crime Survey. London: *Home Office research study 197*

relation to education: those with higher education and those with least formal education tend to try drugs in greater proportions than do those in the middle educational groupings. However, a notable exception to this is heroin, which tends to be found most in the least advantaged groups in society.

Cannabis is the most commonly used illicit drug in British society. National surveys ask if people have 'ever taken' a substance and if so, whether they have done so in the last week, month or year. National surveys suggest that approximately a quarter of people in Britain under the age of sixty have 'ever taken' this substance and that just under half of all young people under the age of twenty-four have done so. Cannabis began to become more widely available about a generation ago, particularly among that generation of students. Current surveys suggest that those in education are still a group with a higher consumption pattern (with one recent study suggesting that approximately one fifth use it within a year[25]).

In the population as a whole, surveys indicate that about a tenth of young people under the age of twenty-nine have 'ever' tried ecstasy, cocaine, LSD or magic mushrooms and about a fifth have tried amphetamines. Recent use (in the last year) tends to be lower, at rates between two per cent and six per cent.

3. Substance use – what were the general findings of the Quaker study?

The general results of the Quaker study were of moderate to low consumption. As regards alcohol, Friends in the study seem to have similar rates of abstinence from alcohol to those of people in

---

[25] Webb, E., Ashton, C.H., Kelly, P., Kamall, F. (1996) Alcohol and Drug Use in UK University Students, *The Lancet* 348:922-25

the population generally. As regards the amount and the frequency
of drinking, the level of consumption in the survey appears to be
generally low. During the week of the survey about a third of
those participating drank no alcohol, and sixty-five per cent of
Quaker men and eighty per cent of Quaker women would be
classed as having 'low' levels of consumption.

Current use of nicotine appears particularly low in comparison
with what might be expected in the general population, taking into
account age, gender and social factors. Older Friends appear to
have smoked in their earlier lives but not to have done so since. As
in the general population, the highest levels were among young
Friends under the age of twenty-four and rates were roughly equal
among Quaker men and women. However, the rate of smoking is
low, even among Young Friends, by national standards (in the
sample less than a fifth of Quakers of this age in the study smoke).

As regards illicit drugs, some experience was found in the Quaker
study, though generally at relatively low levels. Cannabis was the
most likely illicit drug to have been tried. Some youthful use of
cannabis by Friends now in their middle years also emerged from
the study (information was not taken as to whether they were
Quakers at the time). This reflects the general social pattern of
the 1960s and 1970s, when such use occurred more widely among
people in further education.

Recent or frequent experience of illicit drugs was not common in
the survey, though it did occur for some, mainly in relation to
cannabis. Comparisons with general figures are particularly
difficult with small numbers, but it seems that cannabis use is
roughly commensurate with the results of other studies of young
people from similar backgrounds (cited above). Experience of
other drugs was lower and tended to be less recent, suggesting
experimentation or occasional behaviour. Although the numbers

were small, amongst those who tried these substances there seemed to be a greater acceptance of 'natural' drugs like cannabis and magic mushrooms, and a greater mistrust of synthesised chemicals. Experience of opiates was not found. There was also a correlation between having tried illicit drugs and nicotine use – this again is found in the general population.

Although Friends in the sample tended to be generally light in their consumption, this is not to say that no higher use occurred, or that Friends are a group without concerns or problems with substances. No 'very high' or 'hazardous' alcohol consumption emerged in the study (in the Department of Health criteria), but intoxication was reported and a small number responded to questions indicating that drinking had caused them some form of stress at some time during the previous year. Some higher levels of alcohol consumption did occur – in the form of 'single occasion' drinking and higher than weekly 'safe drinking' limits. This was mainly but by no means exclusively among younger people. A small number of Friends reported psychological or physical reliance, most commonly on nicotine: alcohol and cannabis were also reported to cause feelings of reliance in a small number. Dependency – or a feeling that this may be a possibility – was cited as a reason for desisting from the use of these substances in particular. Some Friends who are now abstinent reported previous dependency on alcohol. The medicinal use of cannabis to relieve pain and other symptoms of illness was also reported.

4. Friends' attitudes to substances

Whilst moderate alcohol use was generally seen as non-problematic, many Friends were strongly aware of its risks in terms of addiction and social problems. Its accepted status in society generally was commented on by some Friends:

*... it's so socially acceptable – when does regular use slip
into alcoholism? How do you define that? Also, I
remember years ago, in Sweden I think, that the
government worked out all the costs of alcohol – on work
and health – liver problems, for example. That made a
strong impression on me.*

There were concerns expressed about the potential of alcohol to
increase aggression, which were related to more general Quaker
values about peace and nonviolence. Conversely, the perception
that cannabis was unlikely to cause such problems made it more
acceptable to some Friends in these terms at least: this drug's
harm tended to be considered in terms of physical and mental
health, spiritual effects, or related to its legal status.

At the time of the study, cannabis had not yet been re-classified as
a Class C drug. It was beyond the scope of the study to explore
issues of legality, but the opportunity was taken to gain some sense
of Friends' perspectives. A majority of Friends in the study
thought there was a case for cannabis to be legalised, but the
majority also thought that the existing law should be observed.
Some Friends also said the illegality of this substance was at least
one of their reasons for not trying it.

Attitudes to nicotine tended to be quite strongly negative –
sometimes amongst those who smoke as well as amongst those
who do not. Part of this concern relates to dependency, of which
there was some experience in all age groups. There were also
concerns about the ethics of the supply chain in relation to
nicotine and illicit substances. A quarter of Friends cited this as a
reason for not smoking nicotine and for a third this was also a
factor in non-use of cannabis. Health factors were more to the
fore in relation to other illicit drugs.

5. Gambling: what are the general patterns in society?

Within society generally, there is a wide diversity in behaviour
according to gambling type. About two thirds of the population
take part in the National Lottery during the course of a year.
Twenty-two per cent buy scratch-cards during that period. Other
forms of gambling (fruit machines, horses and private betting)
stand between about eleven and fifteen percent, while the figure
for the pools is a little less. Involvement in gambling assessed on
'last week' figures is much lower, with forty-seven per cent of the
population having played the National Lottery during this
period, and other forms of gambling all below ten per cent.[26] The
buying of raffle tickets does not form part of national survey
material.

On the whole, men tend to gamble more than women, even on the
National Lottery, at which figures are slightly more even. People
between sixteen and twenty-four and those over the age of
seventy-five are least likely to play the National Lottery and
people over sixty-five are least likely to undertake most forms of
gambling except bingo. Younger people under twenty-four who
gamble are most likely to play slot machines and to use scratch-
cards.

People in full-time education show low rates of gambling and
people in the most advantaged social groupings are the least likely
of all the social classes to gamble. However, people in the most
advantaged social classes had higher rates of participation in
visiting casinos, while the tendency is reversed in the case of
bingo. Social and economic factors seem to have little relationship

---

[26] Orford, O., Sprosten, K., Erens, B., White, L., and Michell, L. (2004),
Gambling and Problem Gambling in Britain. Brunner-Routledge (figures taken
from British Gambling Survey).

with horse-racing and slot-machine play. While betting stakes do not vary very strongly, people with low incomes tend to stake a higher percentage of their income.[27]

6. What were the results of the Quaker study as regards gambling?

Within the Quaker study, nearly two thirds of respondents stated that in general terms, they do take part in fund-raising raffles and feel comfortable about doing so. Just over a third did not. There were no significant differences according to age or gender.

The study showed that some participation in other forms of gambling did take place, but was markedly lower than might be expected from general population norms taking into account gender, age and the usual socio-economic factors. About thirty per cent of those participating said that they had 'ever' bought a National Lottery ticket and under a tenth of Friends in the sample had played the National Lottery in the previous year: national figures are approximately sixty per cent for play within the year. Recent participation in the 'last week' was less than one percent. Any other form of betting was rare, with no 'last week' participation and very little in the last year.

---

[27] Orford et al., 2004, page 155

CHAPTER 3
SPIRITUALITY, SUBSTANCE USE
AND GAMBLING

1. Perspectives from the study

Friends who participated in the study were asked what kinds of
connections, if any, they made between substance use and
gambling and their spiritual lives. The study reveals – perhaps not
surprisingly – that there is a very wide variety amongst Friends as
regards approaches to spiritual life. There were also difficulties in
trying to pose questions and render spiritual meanings in words.
However, impact on spiritual life emerged as an important factor
for Friends when they considered whether or how to use
substances. Spirituality was also important for Friends in relation
to gambling – though in a slightly different way.

The general sense that emerged from the study about the
connections between substance use, gambling and spiritual life
can be summarised in the words of one Friend:

Everything affects my spiritual life and is affected by it.

Spirituality was most often described by the Friends who
participated in the research as being about connectedness – to
self, to others, to the natural world, or to God (however defined).
The majority of respondents felt the use of substances or

gambling could interfere with this connection – and the study suggests that this perspective lies behind the moderate or abstinent behaviour of most of those who participated.

For some, an important factor in spiritual connectedness is being able to think and discern clearly – substance use might interfere with this:

> *Non-use means I am clearer in my thinking and making a choice in 'Free Will'.*

> *I am sure that using cannabis would confuse me (and I'm pretty confused already!)*

> *It's important to me to be clear and consistent and to be myself – and non-substance use is part of this.*

> *Non-use – less clouded inner light – hopefully!*

> *I think it would affect one's thinking, reasoning, discernment and thus one's spiritual life.*

For many Friends, the relationship with God was central to this feeling:

> *The clearer my consciousness, the more alive I feel and receptive to God's wisdom.*

> *I believe 'wholeness' and being your 'real' self is the state in which you can connect with God. I feel substances can change my 'real' self.*

For most, this perspective was a reason for limiting alcohol use. It was also shared by some who had tried other substances but had arrived at a similar point:

> *I am not sure I can distinguish [between spiritual considerations and being a Quaker]. It's about God – and because my spiritual God-life has always been part and*

parcel of being a Quaker... I can't distinguish the two,
but it's very much about the relationship with God... It
goes back to the "body as temple" idea. How can I be
fully related to God if in some ways I am escaping by
smoking cannabis?

A relationship with God was also related to gambling by some
Friends. One Friend's words express this feeling:

... if you're trying to win it's something material, you're
not responding to God. Unfounded hope, anxiety and
anticipation are not what God would want... at least for
me... gambling is very much a spiritual issue...

For the small number who did gamble, however, there could be a
different outlook:

Gambling once or twice a year – it doesn't feel as though it
comes between me and my spirituality.

While most Quakers in the study felt substance use was not helpful
spiritually, for a few Friends in some particular situations – often
involving the natural world – spiritual connectedness had
sometimes been enhanced by cannabis use:

...at night in the long summer evenings, the stars were
out, it was windy... that was spiritually enhancing...

I'm not at all sure about what my spirituality is, and am
sometimes wary of talking about these things – it feels
like a very personal thing – but I have sometimes had that
sense of connection with the world or other people when
I've been stoned – and so that is where I feel there is an
affinity between the basis of my spirituality, which I
relate to Quakerism – and substance use.

For most Quakers in the study, spiritual awareness and practice
seemed to be related to a particularly low use of alcohol and of
other substances. However, a belief in God *per se* did not seem
particularly related to either gambling or substance use.

*Pir Vilayat Inayat Khan, the Sufi master, makes the
point that in a jump of the spiritual kind made through
drugs, the experimenter may indeed reach a genuine
insight but has no inward staircase to go up and down, as
does the mystic who has reached the same place by means
of his worshipping silence, good works and grace...*

*This especially underlined for me the need to investigate
to what extent spirituality is a way of life and to what
extent a state of consciousness.*

Damaris Parker-Rhodes, discussing the
aftermath of an occasion in which she
experimentally tried LSD (1977)
Truth: A Path not a Possession
Swarthmore Lecture, London,
Quaker Home Service

For Friends who participated in the study, excess tended to be
construed strongly in spiritual terms, as was the possibility of
dependency:

An overuse of any substance would damage spiritual life.

*Being drunk and spiritual may be confused while
intoxicated, but they are not the same!*

*Dependence on a substance limits growth, because that
substance becomes the most important thing in the world.*

The physical effects of substance use and misuse could be very
much a part of this insight:

> *Anything that harms you physically harms you*
> *spiritually and acts as a barrier to God. I know if I'm*
> *tired or excited or ill, I'm less likely to respond to what*
> *God is asking of me. Experimenting must interfere with*
> *spiritual life. Where misused, drugs are definitely*
> *spiritually damaging.*

When most Friends in the study considered gambling, the activity
itself (rather than excess) tended to be seen as a spiritual matter.
Again, this is connected with the low levels of gambling among
the Friends in the study. Nearly two thirds of those participating
in the survey agreed with the statement that 'gambling works
against spirituality by encouraging materialism' – and those who
agreed with the statement were less likely to have engaged in
gambling than those who did not.

An emphasis on spiritual life does emerge as an important part of
abstinence and moderation for many Friends, though it is also
true to say that occasional substance use – and for a small
number, occasional gambling – had little or no effect on their
sense of connection with nature, with others and with God or
spirit.

Where excess or dependence had occurred, however, a spiritual
dimension was often vital, both for the individual concerned and
for those involved in the process of helping or counselling.

We asked two Friends to explore some of the connections they see
between spiritual life and recovery from addiction. They offer
their reflections in the two pieces that follow.

**2.   Spiritual connections: counselling and dependency – a
          personal perspective**

Give sorrow words: the grief that does not speak
Whispers the o'er-fraught heart and bids it break.

Macbeth – Act 4. Scene III

Shakespeare, as usual, had it right. When I worked for several years as a counsellor in a project for people in recovery from addiction I found that for those I worked with there had been too few words able to be spoken, too many hearts o'er fraught, too many brought to near breaking. In many ways we were blessed as our residents had already survived the rigours (and later the joys) of primary care. They had had time to detoxify, time, in most cases, to acknowledge and accept their huge problems with alcohol, other drugs and in many cases with relationships, food and gambling. By the time they reached us they had at least the beginnings of their lives back; physically much healthier, grateful for the help they had already received and beginning to have a sense of belonging. Life could still be enormously difficult, trying to live with the knowledge of how their lives had been, without reaching again for the longed-for anaesthesia of substances. Not that that comfort had been there in the later stages, their drug of choice, initially so amazing and desirable, becoming instead the nightmare succubus that demanded and promised everything but gave in the end nothing but fear and self-hatred.

Some of our residents would, when they had built up enough trust, describe early lives of abject misery, of neglect and abuse of all kinds. Often the chain of misuse and abuse led back through generations where the 'sins of the fathers' were indeed visited on the sons... and daughters... and grandsons and granddaughters in their turn. God knows in how many generations before. So of what use would it be to demonise parents in that situation? Doing their best perhaps with the meagre and inappropriate tools they had been given for their task? The work for us then was in doing

*what we could, building on work already done, and with the
group of residents providing much of the help and support for
each other, to acknowledge all that there was in each one that
hungered for life, creativity and that most soul-saving gift of
unconditional love. A distinction has to be made all along the way
between the behaviour and the person. Limits and boundaries set
to the one whilst the other can still be accepted and cared for.
Love, as far as is humanly possible, needs to be a constant – not
always easy in what can be a challenging and unpredictable
world.*

*Of course not all of our residents came from such dysfunctional
homes and I would in no way wish to feed the fears of parents or
partners that they had caused the slide into misuse and
dependency. The whole subject is complex and confusing and
sometimes it seems as though a combination of any addictive
substance with a particularly susceptible person would be enough
to trigger major problems. Lack of self-confidence, needing to feel
a 'part of the crowd', feeling, as I have heard it described, that
you have been born 'two drinks short of OK'. Sometimes it seems
all that is needed is the age-old desire to do something your
parents would disapprove of. All or any of these can be enough to
lead people into the 'Wild Wood' – and while the lucky ones find
the path back out again there are all too many who cannot find
their way back to the light.*

*So how do we, as Friends, parents, teachers, overseers, elders,
counsellors, partners, seek to help? I know from my own
experience it is not something to undertake lightly or without
enough good and experienced support. The 'Wild Wood' is indeed
deep and dark and the paths can be devious, deceptive. The 'dis-
ease', if one may be permitted to use that useful but not entirely
proven word, has its own gremlins to 'whisper the o'er fraught*

heart' both of sufferer and carer. Its goal is relapse and the gremlins are its allies. Recovery is rarely all-in-one-go, a straightforward walk into the sunset with a new life. Neither is there a one-size-fits-all path to recovery, though clearly many people find enormous support and a way back with AA, NA and the other Anonymous Fellowships. Whichever path is chosen it is often two steps forward and one step back; occasional slips back into old ways of thinking, sometimes old behaviours. Trust takes time to grow and different ways of being need to be explored. The path is hard both for those who walk it and those who walk beside them, who try to maintain hope, offer information and sometimes need to seek ways to forgive much that has happened in the past.

Working and walking beside those most deeply abused requires us to hear and to hold horrors that we have no wish to hear, except that someone has to – and then we most desperately need our own resources to help with the holding. However careful we are we can still find ourselves paying heavily in some ways. Stress has its day and if we are lucky we can see it coming before it bites too deeply. It is still a privilege to work with people who are willing, for the sake of their souls as well as their bodies, to begin the long hard walk into recovery. A walk that can take years as they first overcome the demands of the addiction itself – and later perhaps find the courage to work through the griefs of their early life that came so near to destroying them. The 'Wild Wood' is deep, but there are maps and there are candles. We have ears to hear and hearts to care. Just for one day at a time.

---

3. Spiritual connections: Quakerism and recovery from addiction –
    a personal perspective

I ended up in hospital having narrowly survived a suicide attempt
at the end of twenty-five years' drinking. The psychiatrist who
saw me before I was discharged suggested I should attend
Alcoholics Anonymous (AA). I was scared that if I drank again I
would die, so I did what he said. The AA group I joined after
leaving hospital met at a Quaker Meeting House. There was a
poster on the notice board that spoke to my condition. It said a
silent Meeting for Worship can be, 'a quiet process of healing',
and, 'a journey of discovery'. I went to my first Meeting for
Worship in September 1984.

Bill W., AA's co-founder, wrote to a Quaker correspondent in 1950:

> The really amazing fact about AA is that all religions see
> in our programme a resemblance to themselves. For
> example, Catholic theologians declare our Twelve Steps to
> be in exact accord with their Ignatian Exercises for
> Retreat, and, though our book (The Big Book – AA's
> basic text) reeks of sin, sickness and death, the Christian
> Science Monitor has often praised it editorially. Now,
> looking through Quaker eyes, you, too, see us favourably.
> What happy circumstances these!'

The longer I attended AA meetings and Quaker Meetings for
Worship I, too, was struck by the similarities between the
fellowship of ex-drunks I had joined and the Religious Society of
Friends.

Here are the first three Steps of AA's suggested programme of
recovery from alcoholism:

> 1. We admitted we were powerless over alcohol – that our
>   lives had become unmanageable;

2. *Came to believe that a Power greater than ourselves could restore us to sanity;*

3. *Made a decision to turn our will and lives over to the care of God* **as we understood Him.**

Compare that with George Fox's inspired insight into the nature of addiction:

Friends, whatever ye are addicted to, the tempter will come in that thing; and when he can trouble you, then he gets advantage over you, and then you are gone. Stand still in that which is pure, after ye see yourselves; and then mercy comes in. After thou seest thy thoughts, and the temptations, do not think, but submit; and then power comes. Stand still in the Light and submit to it, and the other will be hushed and gone; and then content comes.

Quaker Faith and Practice 20.42

To begin with, I loved **getting** drunk – but I hated **being** a drunk. I tried all I knew to stop or control my drinking, but those grimly determined and eventually desperate efforts always ended in failure, until I reached a state of 'pitiful and incomprehensible demoralisation', as the *Big Book* says. It was only when I gave up the unequal fight that I gained relief. I had to surrender to win – to stand still in the Light and submit – then power came. Jo Farrow experienced a similar rock-bottom experience that got her attention (though it didn't involve booze). In *The World in my Heart* she recounts:,

If we are fortunate, as I was, there may be a crisis so devastating that only a kind of dying and beginning again can enable us to make sense of the experience and learn from it.

That's what happened to me.

Steps Four and Five emphasise the importance of identifying what was wrong with us and bringing it into the light.

4. *We made a searching and fearless moral inventory of ourselves;*

5. *We admitted to God, to ourselves and to another human being the exact nature of our wrongs'. (Step 10 – 'We continued to take personal inventory and when we were wrong promptly admitted it', continues the process as a daily discipline).*

As a drunk I felt ashamed and guilty, but was unable to tell anyone. In Steps 4 and 5 I was finally able to be honest with myself and to share my darkest secrets with an understanding human being, in my case my AA sponsor. Friends also know how vital this act of kenosis – emptying – can be.

> *Careful listening is fundamental to helping each other; it goes beyond finding out about needs and becomes part of meeting them. Some would say it is the single most useful thing that we can do. Those churches that have formal confession understand its value, but confession does not have to be formal to bring benefits. Speaking the unspeakable, admitting the shameful, to someone who can be trusted and who will accept you in love as you are, is enormously helpful.*
>
> *Quaker Faith and Practice* 12.01

In Steps six and seven we become *'entirely ready to have God remove all our defects of character',* **and** *'humbly ask Him to remove our shortcomings'.*

In the next two Steps we set out to repair the wreckage of the past:

> *Step 8: We made a list of all persons we had harmed and became willing to make amends to them all;*
>
> *Step 9: We made direct amends to such people wherever possible, except when to do so would injure them or others.*

Or, as Friends are urged,

> *Where any have received offence from any other, first speak privately to the party concerned, and endeavour reconciliation between themselves; and not to whisper or aggravate matters against them behind their backs, to the making parties, and the breach wider.*
>
> Quaker Faith and Practice 20.70

Bill W. called Step II the 'growth Step' – practising this Step empowers us to grow spiritually into the person we are meant to be:

> *We sought through prayer and meditation to improve our conscious contact with God **as we understood Him**, praying only for knowledge of His will for us and the power to carry that out.*

Advices and Queries endorse this approach:

> *Do you try to set aside times of quiet for openness to the Holy Spirit? All of us need to find a way into silence which allows us to deepen our awareness of the divine and to find the inward source of our strength. Seek to know an inward stillness, even amid the activities of daily life. Do you encourage in yourself and in others a habit of dependence on God's guidance for each day?*
>
> Quaker Faith and Practice 1.02

One of AA's sayings is, 'To keep it we have to give it away.' (As in,

*'Heal the sick, cleanse the lepers, raise the dead, cast out demons.
Freely ye have received, freely give'*– Matthew 10.8).

Step 12 says:

> *Having had a spiritual awakening as the result of these
> Steps (1-11), we tried to carry this message to alcoholics,
> and to practise these principles in all our affairs.*

William Penn said of early Friends,

> *They were changed men themselves before they went about
> to change others. Their hearts were rent as well as their
> garments, and they knew the power and work of God
> upon them... and as they freely received what they had to
> say from the Lord, so they freely administered it to others.*
>
> Quaker Faith and Practice 19.48

Like Friends, AA does not set out to convert or proselytise; John
Barleycorn is our recruiting sergeant. AA is a programme of
attraction, rather than promotion. The logical answer to the
question 'What must I do?' is 'You must do this (that, or the
other).' AA answers the question tangentially. *The Big Book* says,

> *If you are an alcoholic who wants to get over it, you may
> already be asking – What do I have to do? It is the
> purpose of this book to answer such questions specifically.*
> **We shall tell you what we have done** *(emphasis added)*.

AA's recovery programme is a report of action taken; it is
descriptive, not prescriptive. We don't tell, we show. There are no
musts, no credal hoops to jump through, no 'authorities' to obey.

> *Dearly beloved Friends, these things we do not lay upon
> you as a rule or form to walk by, but that all, with the
> measure of light which is pure and holy, may be guided;*

and so in the light walking and abiding, these may be fulfilled in the Spirit, not from the letter, for the letter killeth, but the Spirit giveth life.

Postscript to an epistle to the
'brethren in the north' issued by a
Meeting of elders of Balby, 1656.
Quaker Faith and Practice 1.01

CHAPTER 4
FRIENDS' EXPERIENCES

1. Stages and changes

The study included adult Friends of all ages, from eighteen to
ninety. Some participants had their formative years during the
1920s and 30s, while others grew up during the 1980s. The social
changes during this period in relation to both substances and
gambling have been considerable.

One Friend, now an octogenerian, who came from a Quaker
family, remembers the approach at home exemplified in an
experience as a young child:

> *My parents were teetotal ...except in the sideboard there
> were bottles and one day I opened it up and thought I'd
> have a sip of all the bottles – oh, well anyone would think
> I was going to hell the next day! It was terrible, terrible.
> And they were totally against gambling. In fact, if you
> were enjoying yourself, you must be doing something
> wrong. It was appalling – and all in the name of God...*

Another Friend of older years who participated in the study
commented:

> *My parents were both teetotallers and Quakers and*
> *abstinence was seen as a virtue. I rebelled against this a*
> *little but see having a strong attitude as quite important*
> *for some people.*

Dorothy Steere, in *Quaker Faith and Practice* 22.62 says:

> *There is little question that if as a parent we have not*
> *taken the time to really listen to children when they are*
> *young, listened not only to their words but to their feelings*
> *behind the words, they are unlikely to want to come with*
> *their sharing in life. Learning to listen to each other in*
> *families can help to make us better listeners to others and*
> *to the Inner Guide.*

Another older participant in the study had perspectives from
childhood that have continued to influence her current conduct:

> *My husband (non-Quaker) and I were fully teetotal for*
> *most of our life and still are in front of grandchildren,*
> *and even now in old age drink very little – he some cider*
> *three or four times a year, me, wine a bit more often...My*
> *husband's grandfather was an addict and wrecked my*
> *mother-in-law's childhood: and my father drank too much*
> *at times. So we are both aware of the 'slippery slope'.*

Another middle-aged Friend felt that a Quaker childhood and
education had given the basis both for framing a personal
position, and for explaining it:

> *It gave me...a language – perhaps structure is the right*
> *word. You could explain to other people why you were*
> *doing or not doing something – because you've got the*
> *vocabulary. I think that's very important in anything, is*
> *giving them vocabulary to say what they want to say.*

Kenneth Barnes, who was a Quaker head-teacher, expresses the
Quaker belief in a spiritual presence that is there for all to draw
on when necessary:

> *We cannot hope to transfer more than a little of our*
> *wisdom to our young people – if wisdom it is... We have*
> *increasingly to stand back as they grow older, knowing*
> *that the problem is passing out of our hands..... Parents*
> *cannot help being anxious, but they must bear that in*
> *themselves, not project it. They cannot live their children's*
> *lives for them.... It is also the moment for parents to tell*
> *themselves that their children are not alone. They are in*
> *the hands of God. God does not offer any kind of*
> *perfection in the actual circumstances of life, nor freedom*
> *from exposure to evil.*
>
> *Quaker Faith and Practice 22.70*

The study showed that Quakers now in middle life were more
likely to drink some alcohol than those of the previous generation
– and also to have had more experience of alcohol during their
younger years. One commented:

> *I might have occasionally got a bit tiddly as a youngster,*
> *but it was unintentional and very infrequent.*

Those who felt that their upbringing had been overly stringent
sometimes made modifications to parental 'messages' in their
middle years – as the octagenerian Friend described:

> *I'd never been to a book-maker or anything but my*
> *husband and I used to have great fun working out a*
> *scheme and watching the television and betting on horses*
> *between ourselves... great fun – very exciting!'*

Some Friends of this middle generation had also tried cannabis in their youth, or had moved in circles (for example, at university) where others did so. Such experiences did not tend to persist (as is indeed the case for the general population) and current use of alcohol tended to be light. However, pressures of work or family responsibilities to both older and younger family members could be sources of stress at this stage and have an impact on substance use. One Friend, for example, described a decision to leave a highly paid but highly stressful job, feeling that a habit of drinking alcohol most evenings as a way of de-stressing was a symptom that their life was out of kilter. Although not widespread, alcohol consumption above recommended health limits at this stage of life could also take place for reasons of enjoyment or sociability.

The experience of some Quakers in this middle generation disposed them to appreciate that experimentation with alcohol or cannabis among young people was not unlikely and need not be catastrophic. However, this could result in issues for some Friends in their role as parents. There was a desire to be open and approachable about such matters without appearing too casual – and there were sometimes uncertainties in approaching the subject in a Quaker context.

One Friend of this generation commented:

> *It's interesting how unconnected these issues feel to Quakerism. I noticed this particularly as my daughter was growing up – all sorts of burning issues re peace testimony, environment and vegetarianism – none regarding drink or drugs. Most of her generation partook (and partake) without any hesitation, though they have mostly (but not all) moderated their use as they've matured. Many of them kept their use hidden from their parents. I used to wonder if I should say anything about*

'*alcohol, drugs and Quakers*' *but there was nothing to hand and it seemed stuffy and counterproductive to do so.* Uncertainties could also be felt by parents who had little direct experience of substances themselves, but appreciated the increased choices – and pressures – on the current generation of young people. In *Quaker Faith and Practice* 22.66, Rosalind Priestman writes that the

> *development of personality is a continuing process – never completed... teenagers begin to realise themselves as separate and different from their parents and friends. It is no easy task to live up to ideals and at the same time to accommodate rival claims and impulses. It is at this time that Quaker children often experience particular difficulties in adjusting to a world beyond their own home where values, standards and expectations are different from those they have grown up with. Do we try to understand the difficulties, stresses and failures of growing children and make them fully aware that, come what may, they are still loved? This does not mean that we give them unlimited licence. They still need an adequate framework within which it is safe to experiment and rebel.*

This study did not involve Friends below eighteen years of age, so the direct perspective of younger teenagers is not represented. Some Young Friends close to that age group felt it was not a strong issue for them, but one younger participant commented:

> *There seems to be an unfortunate tendency among Quakers to think that we are not as affected by the problems of drinking and drug taking, that we are somehow above such things. This seems to me, from my own experience and that of Quaker friends, to be both misguided and dangerous.*
>
> respondent under 24 years of age.

We are encouraged in *Advices and Queries* not to let social
pressures influence our decisions – but the trends in wider society
are likely to affect us to some degree and we cannot fail to be
influenced by our peer group and friends. Whilst the study
suggests that the behaviour of younger Friends is generally non-
problematic, some Young Friends also reported that their
behaviour could go through many changes during their teens and
twenties. Experimentation and movement between use, higher use
and abstinence did occur for some, principally in relation to
alcohol, and more occasionally, cannabis.

> *I've never been a really heavy drinker, but on occasions
> I have got quite drunk and felt very unwell as a result...
> That was something very much about being at university,
> I think that it was actually very good for me to go through
> that for me to have a bit of a reckless time or done some
> reckless things and see what they did to me...*

> *I was teetotal for about nine months. My attitude now is
> that I won't drink to excess and as soon as I get to the
> point where I start to feel the effects on my brain, then
> I know that I have had enough and don't have any more.*

Relationships could be very much a part of these processes...

> *Cannabis was time out...It certainly used to be, but it's
> less so now ... I had a friend who very much was a
> smoker and I would go and spend three days with her and
> spend most of the time having sex and smoking and that
> was very much time out, relaxation. She would say that
> too...I do feel what I'm working towards is not using any
> substance – and I get there sometimes...*

For many younger Friends, relating to a mixed social circle
involves developing selectivity and judgement:

*...some of my best friends do go out drinking with the
intention of getting drunk – it's not impressive – I will
not go out with them at all on that occasion, or I'll leave
early. I have a bit, given the context of whatever social
event I'm at, but that's what I want to do and I'm
comfortable in myself about that. The friends who are
into drinking more, that's put me off becoming close to
them. So my closest friends I would say have similar
attitudes to alcohol as I do.*

Anne Hosking has pointed out that:

*If we, the important adults in their lives, respect their
integrity, their capacity to worship and experience God,
then they (our children) will respect it too. If we share
the skills that we are learning, then they will practise them
too.*

Quaker Faith and Practice 22.71

2. Experiences of problems or dependency

Some Friends reported either having experienced a problem with
substances or gambling themselves, or having been affected by
dependency in the family. Such issues affected all age groups:

*When I took LSD I thought I had gone to hell and had to
gradually build up my 'spirituality' again with the help
of anti-psychotic drugs, etc.*

*I have suffered physical abuse as a direct result of alcohol
use.*

*My father was an addictive gambler on the horses which
went hand in hand with alcohol. I only discovered this in
my teens – and what a struggle my mother had had.*

Within the younger age group, dependency was most likely to be reported on nicotine. Some younger Friends in mid to late twenties reported difficulties with tobacco (usually having started smoking in their teens):

> *I would stop smoking if I could...*

Friends in the older age groups in the survey also spoke of previous dependency on nicotine, at a time before the health consequences were established.

Cannabis was also experienced as likely to cause reliance.

> *I was actually into pot for about 2¹/₂ years. I got over it sorted it out and went back and just did it socially. Pot is incredibly addictive... When I stopped, it wasn't the only thing – I was unhappy about my life at the time. I decided that was the main reason...*

Amongst older Friends, there was some past experience of alcohol dependency:

> *From being a dirty broken Alcoholic I prayed to Jesus to help me and as long as I remain clean I have a rich, full life.*

A few Friends – usually in middle-age or older – reported that they had experienced problems with prescribed medication:

> *I became physically dependent on painkillers I took while suffering from arthritis. It was difficult to stop once the arthritis subsided – but through perseverance and sheer stubbornness not to let it get the better of me, was able to overcome this. It was a painful experience I would prefer not to repeat.*

> *By chance I was advised at the chemist how to break the habit of taking temazepam every night.*

> *I felt I developed dependency on prescribed medication,*
> *and 'tailed off gradually'.*

Some of these Friends commented on a lack of information about the potential for dependency at the time of prescription (though it is also the case that some of these were not recent experiences).

Problem use and dependency in close others – either friends or family – had been experienced by nearly fifteen per cent of Friends in the study. This affected Friends of all ages, and such problems could often be long-term. One Friend shares her experience of addiction in the family.

A Quaker mother shares her experience of addiction in the family:

What is it like to be the mother of a drug addict? It's like being on a see saw – a sickening see saw of huge mood swings. Today R (now aged 26) has just rung from a prison; he has been 'nicked for theft' again. I feel relief that he is still alive and is sounding quite calm and rational, probably not under the influence of heroin at the moment. There is a spark of hope for the future again. But during the last four and a half weeks, during which he has been out of contact since walking out of a residential rehabilitation unit, I have felt dejected, depressed, worried, angry, sad. Dejected and depressed because this awfulness and unpredictability has been going on for some ten years now. Worried because he has been extremely ill and hospitalised as a result of his drug taking in the last year and I worry for his immediate safety and his long term health. Angry because a part of me still cannot really understand how a young man with so much in his favour can throw his life away in such pointlessness when others who have far fewer advantages can overcome their difficulties and lead happy and worthwhile lives. Most of all, I am sad because I know he is lonely and unhappy, as he reveals on the odd occasions he is prepared to talk to us.

And yet, I can understand that it probably all stems from the first two and a half years of his life, before he came to us as a pre-adoption foster child (we were allowed to adopt him after a year and a half probationary period) and from the neglect and instability he experienced in those years. I feel frustrated and angry with myself as his adoptive mother, with all of us in the immediate and wider family, with the adoption services and with R himself that none of us, separately or together, could overcome the deep hurt of rejection and the loss of self esteem engendered by those early experiences. Hindsight is a wonderful thing and my husband and I did not help ourselves or R, I now feel, by always thinking we had not got it right as adoptive parents. This left us with a burden of guilt that has been hard to throw off and has meant that we have not always dealt with R in the wisest way in latter years. The authorities always maintained that all he needed was love in a family that already had a child, but we have often felt that what was really needed was a lot more guidance in dealing with a child who turned out to have special psychological needs. Did we all try hard enough? Was this descent into drug taking an inevitable path?

I cannot say that being a Quaker initially came very much to the forefront of the experience. Except, perhaps, that I have needed a lot of patience and a calm, steady, consistent approach. These might be seen as Quakerly attributes and have had to be worked at when set against the emotions listed above.

Certainly, I derived a lot of comfort from knowing that we were held in the thoughts of the Meeting's prayer group week by week. One elderly Friend, who has since died, used to ask me straight away each Sunday morning and whenever we met how R was getting on and what the latest news was. Fred could not DO anything, of course, none of us could it seemed, but how uplifting it was to know that a man of such Quakerly spirit concerned himself with R and his family. When R eventually entered residential rehab recently, I just wished I could have phoned Fred and told him something a bit more positive than the habitual news of prison or life on the streets.

I did not ever approach overseers and ask for any kind of help from the Meeting. Although I had been a member of the Society for 30 years at that point, it did not seem right to present the Meeting with my personal and family problems, especially as I was not a very regular attender after I married, being the only Quaker in the family.

The only thing that I did wonder about for a while was whether we could get R into a Quaker boarding school for the last few years of his school life as he was failing at the local comprehensive, academically and socially, long before drugs were part of his difficulties. His father and I thought the Quaker ethos might make a difference, but we would have needed bursary help and, in the end, the overriding factor in our decision not to pursue this idea was the fear that R would react badly if he saw this as a 'putting away' rather than a helpful new opportunity. The fact that he is our adopted son and that we have an older, natural born son was a strong factor in this decision.

Much later on, I started reading $QAADRANT$[28] and was urged by a member of Monthly Meeting who knew of my family situation to contact QAAD for advice and guidance. I have been so glad that I did. At this point, we already knew the full extent of

---

[28] The quarterly magazine issued by QAAD

R's heroin and crack cocaine use and had spent several years visiting him in prisons in many locations when he had been convicted of drugs related thefts. We had talked to various probation officers, prison officers, solicitors and hostel workers over the years, but the advice from QAAD has been really helpful.

Neither my husband nor I feel we can do much for R except to always be there when he wants us and to let him know that we always love him whatever he does. We have learned from bitter experience not to fall for his demands for money, nor for his carefully couched tales that pull at the heartstrings. We are now learning that 'tough love' as it is called, means not helping him out even though he seems so immature and helpless as he is very 'street wise' and needs to take the next step of standing completely on his own feet if he is going to make any real progress and finally free himself of his addictive tendencies. Will he eventually take the road back – and how many more years will it take?

> Respect the wide diversity among us in our lives and relationships. Refrain from making prejudiced judgments about the life journeys of others. Do you foster the spirit of mutual understanding and forgiveness which our discipleship asks of us? Remember that each of us is unique, previous, a child of God.
>
> Advice in *Advices and Queries* 1.02 22:

CHAPTER 5
THE TESTIMONIES

*... testimonies are not pragmatic responses to the spirit of
the age, being neither political principles nor
programmes, but the outcome of the Quaker religious
tradition, the greater whole against which they have to be
evaluated and practised.*[29]

John Punshon

1. What do these testimonies mean to Friends?

The testimony[30] on substance use is designated 'moderation and
abstinence' in *Quaker Faith and Practice* – words that cover both
of the historical meanings of 'temperance.' Given that this
testimony has not generally been as prominent as that on
gambling (and still less so than the peace testimony, for example)
part of the aim of this study was to discover how important this
testimony is for Friends in a modern context – and what the

[29] Punshon, J. (1990) *Testimony and Tradition*, Swarthmore Lecture, London:
Headley Brothers Ltd. p 19
[30] 'Testimony' is a Quaker term for a value or belief that is lived out by Quakers
in their daily lives. Other examples of Quaker testimonies relate to peace, truth
and integrity, equality and simplicity.

testimonies on substance use and gambling mean to us in principle and in practice.

Many Friends, when asked about a Quaker approach to substance use, defined it in terms of moderation, as one participant succinctly put it: *'avoiding excess'*. However, moderation and abstinence were often considered not only in terms of consumption, but also related to other Quaker testimonies – particularly simplicity and truth – and to broader Quaker values:

> ... *respect for self and others, simple life-style; these things [substances] not needed.*

> *Moderate truthful lifestyle I try to follow derives from Quakerism.*

> ...*being kind to myself and others in the long term.*

> ...*spiritual/physical sense of balance; health in the widest sense*

Interestingly, in view of Quaker history, moderation did not involve a strongly ascetic sense for many Friends. For those who drank alcohol – that is, the majority of Friends who participated in the study – the reason most frequently cited for doing so was 'for enjoyment' (with sociability being the next most common reason). Enhancement (wine with a meal, for example) was also mentioned. Thus, pleasure as a motive seemed to be acceptable to most Friends – and was more likely to be so to younger Friends.

One Friend took this a stage further and mused on the ascetic tradition in relation to intoxication:

> *It is difficult to disentangle the historical attitude against intoxication from the equally historical attitudes to things I value highly – e.g. music, theatre, enjoyable dress, the pleasures of the senses.*

However, this was not a perspective shared by the majority of Friends in the study, who generally considered substance use as undesirable because it impairs self-control or results in intoxication – and this was equally true of Young Friends. It seems that for the majority of Friends, some ascetic attitudes are present, but as was predominantly the case with spiritual considerations, these are directed at excess.

This is a similar perspective to that expressed by one of the respondents in the book *Role Over*:

> *personally, I don't understand the testimony against gambling or drinking – I don't see that these are in essence immoral acts. The problem is not the act itself but the phenomenon of addiction and the effect the act has on the individual. I think our testimony would be better expressed as a testimony for 'avoiding the dangerous occasions of sin'.*[31]

However, another Friend quoted in the same publication expresses a perspective that has an ascetic 'training' dimension. Aware of the dilemma of refusing to take part in charity lotteries, s/he nevertheless felt that

> *as athletes exercise their muscles to be at their best, so grappling with problems of all kinds should help one's spiritual growth. It's no good just giving up and dying spiritually.*[32]

Within this study, few Friends seemed personally drawn to gamble, so issues of enjoyment or pleasure arose infrequently. However, for those Friends who did take part in any gambling,

---

[31] *Role Over?*, London: Quaker Books, 2004, 4.1
[32] *Role Over?*, 4.11

enjoyment or 'fun' was often one of the main motivations.

As was the case with substance use, the testimony against gambling was linked by many Friends to other Quaker testimonies and concerns – most commonly those of equality and justice.

> ...the whole gambling set up is about taking away money from poor people. So it does interact with my sense of social conscience...

> {It relates to} our social testimony i.e. 'taxes on the poor'

This perspective was often related particularly to the National Lottery:

> It encourages poorer people to gamble money they haven't got.

Within the context of National Lottery funding for charitable or valuable purposes, another Friend expresses the issues thus:

> the point of a testimony against gambling, or alcohol or whatever, is to abstain from something which could cause great harm, in order to show that (a) it IS possible to live happily without it, (b) it is God's will that we set an example of living without it, (c) we can be seen, by the people who are in the grip of addiction, or whose lives are blighted by someone else's addiction, as people who have noticed them. If we deny ourselves something fun, in order to witness to God's leading, we achieve the above. If we deny other people things they need, it starts being a bit self-righteous.[33]

---

[33] *Role Over?*, 4.13

2. What guides us?

The study indicated that Quakers who took part in the study
mainly did not undertake gambling and were generally moderate
in their approach to substance use – but this still left questions
about how – and even whether – the testimonies have a direct
influence on Friends' attitudes or behaviour. Responses among
Friends had many strands.

For those brought up as Quakers (the majority amongst Young
Friends General Meeting), the testimony on gambling often
formed an early form of guidance, which is tested against later
life experience. One Young Friend stated:

> *I remember that my parents disapproved – and I grew up
> in a seaside resort which has various slot machines – you
> know, at the pier and so on. I never felt drawn to go into
> these and I always disliked it when I ever went in with
> friends...*

Another said:

> *I do identify quite strongly with the Advices and I do
> think that's where my initial dislike and mistrust of the
> idea of gambling came from... During my work in a
> community centre...I saw lots of people with addiction
> issues and benefit problems. I saw a couple who had been
> very strongly addicted to gambling...*

Among those who came to Quakerism later in life many felt that
they had 'Quaker values' before they officially joined or became
attenders – and these testimonies were either part of that sense of
belonging or readily assimilated. One such respondent put it like
this:

> *I don't gamble. I've only done the lottery once – I don't
> think I'm directly influenced by Quakerism as such – just
> much more naturally aligned with the Quaker position.*

As regards substance use, a similar natural congruence is the case for many Friends:

> *Decision [to be moderate] made prior to coming to Friends.*

The testimonies: *confirm my own beliefs but I think they should be stronger.*

For another *'they chime with my personal values'*, while for yet another the testimony seems irrelevant, as *'whether Quaker or not, I have no desire to take any drug'*.

Friends in YFGM from non-Quaker families also expressed this easy sense of identification. For many of the Friends who participated in the study, these testimonies seem to reinforce and deepen their values and inclinations, rather than acting as direct influences on personal behaviour.

> *I think it's generally the feeling that there's no need. I mean I have the odd drink, but it's not what I do most of the time. I don't smoke cigarettes, I don't do any sort of substances and it's just something I don't feel I need to do to make my life any better. So in a sense it comes back to Quakerism in a round about way. It's not because I'm a Quaker that I believe it's the right thing to do, but it's one of the things that has informed my way of the world – and my own view is that I can live a happy life without having to resort to drugs, or drink heavily.*

> *I already felt that way about gambling. I felt naturally attuned to what Quakers were saying on that one. I suppose it's also a bit of 'well, I'm not susceptible to that anyway' – really boring virtue…*

This was also apparent in some of the statistics compiled by the study. For example, the most common primary reason for not gambling was given as 'personal disinclination' – but 'Quaker testimony' was the most frequently cited second reason.

However, for some of those in the study, the testimonies do have an influencing effect on behaviour – particularly as regards substance use. This may be at a precautionary level:

> *[The testimony] ...makes me moderate any tendency to drink alcohol regularly... the belief that you don't need to be in an altered state to enjoy life.*

It was also notable that Friends whose circumstances, inclinations or behaviour were not naturally in alignment with one of these testimonies nevertheless felt the testimonies were influential for them. For some, this may mean reducing levels of substance use, illicit use, or excess. One younger Friend reports:

> *[The testimony] makes me decide not to take illegal drugs – one of the reasons. Supports me in this stance. Makes me feel guilty for drinking too much – occasionally stops me getting too drunk – one reason.*

Similarly, for another younger Friend, the ideal of moderation is sometimes difficult to sustain in relation to a range of substances – but the standard nevertheless has a stabilising effect:

> *Yes I'm aware, I try to resist, but I think – it's almost sometimes I feel a bit guilty, but I remind myself Quakerism's not about guilt, I try not to feel that. That's always at the back of my mind. It certainly keeps things under control – I can go a little bit out of control sometimes...*

For this Friend, moderation acts as an ideal that s/he is not able to reach consistently. The testimonies also had an influencing effect on those who are already moderate. A light consumer of alcohol, for example, felt that abstinence would be the Quaker

ideal – and undertook a similar process of reflection about the
testimony:

> ...*if I felt that I was being totally true to Quakerism then
> I would completely need to be teetotal... I'm not sure I
> can say why. ...Quite a lot of what I think about social
> issues in relation to Quakerism is that it is the kind of
> ideal as to how a person – a Quaker – can live their lives
> most in harmony with the world and their spiritualism
> and Quakerism and everything – and I suppose not
> drinking in my mind is more towards that ideal in the
> same way say as buying certain coffee is. So there are lots
> of aspects of my life where I feel that I am doing O.K.
> but there's still a lot of ground between where I am and
> where the ideal would be.*

This kind of process of negotiation happened less frequently with
gambling, but it did occur occasionally:

> *I occasionally play poker with my friends for five pence
> maximum raise... I can imagine a situation where I'm
> gambling for fun, but for other members in the group it's
> something quite serious, then that would be wrong and I
> would not want to be part of that... whilst there are big
> negative aspects of gambling in society at the moment I
> don't feel that I'm contributing to them.*

For another Friend, the inconsistency with testimony is
acknowledged and considered, but put to one side for the present:

> *I give myself a limit... I don't go to win – it's an
> evening's entertainment and I'm willing to lose...
> Quakerism sits outside gambling, it doesn't fit with
> Quakerism. I haven't spent time looking at it, there are a
> lot of steps in there I'm not sure of.*

For these Friends, there was a continuing process of dialogue with
the testimony, prompted by the need to examine divergences with
personal inclination or behaviour. For some Friends who described
changes in behaviour over time, this dialogue with the testimony
was often a factor in the process.

A few participants reported that Quakerism acted as a support in
giving up a substance. One respondent's *'Quakerism underlined
and reinforced my desire to give up smoking'*. Another *'became a
Quaker as a result of practising the 12 steps [of Alcoholics
Anonymous] in my daily life. They are still central to my daily life –
supported by my Quakerism.'* Here the behaviour led to adopting
Quakerism, which in turn supported the behaviour.

3. Personal responsibility and Quaker religious tradition

The variation in approach to testimony was also apparent in the
responses to a question in the written survey, in which Friends
were asked about the idea of 'guidelines' on substance use in
Quakerism. Some Friends felt they *'should be stronger'* or more
obvious. At the other end of the scale some Friends hoped they
would not be affected: *'I make my own opinions'* being an example
of this outlook. However, the majority of Friends focused on the
idea of the written testimony assisting the process of personal
reflection. The following comments are characteristic of many:

> *They make me think!*

> *I consider my use carefully as suggested by Advices and
> Queries.*

> *Prompt me to make a well thought-out choice.*

One Friend who had experienced substance problems before
coming to Quakerism found this atmosphere particularly helpful
and inclusive, and believed it aided the reduction of illicit and
prescribed medication:

> *I do have a firm belief that people take drink and drugs*
> *to keep away from emotions they can't deal with. The*
> *knowledge that it's not forbidden – that it's for me to make*
> *my own choices – I find that very reassuring, a real*
> *lifeline…*

The testimony on substance use is not one of abstinence only, so the process of personal consideration and responsible action regarding use could involve many elements. A similar process occurred in relation to gambling, though for most Friends this tended to focus on decisions about responsible investment. When weighing up individual decisions in particular circumstances, Friends tended to refer to wider Quaker values – some of which recurred like motifs throughout the study. The first of these concerns the power of example.

The idea of example and the impact of personal action are implicit in the Quaker testimony on substance use ('in view of the harms done…') and this element was singled out by several Friends in their definition of testimony: *'moderation, considering above all whether your behaviour negatively affects others.'* Another commented:

> *They chime with my personal values. The one that's extra*
> *(to Quakerism) is to consider the example set by our*
> *behaviour.*

Similarly, when asked if Friends had felt the need to give up a substance and if so, whether their Quakerism had any connection with this decision, one replied:

> *The expectation that others have of the purity of*
> *Quakerism makes me think I should think twice about*
> *public drinking and smoking.*

If testimony is defined as a method of encouraging others to change (*Quaker Faith and Practice* 20.18, quoted below), then it becomes crucial to set a good example.

One respondent wondered whether his/her smoking encouraged other people to do so and conversely whether not smoking helped others:

> *I guess partly to do with being someone who does not smoke and yes, not wanting to be seen as a smoker. Which probably is part of my being a Quaker, and stuff about does your smoking encourage other people to do so, and if I'm not smoking does that help other people or not. But also just the "what's this giving you?" – your conscience is about doing the right thing.*

Another felt that deliberately drinking soft drinks at parties would give others confidence not to give in to peer pressure:

> *If I am in an 'alcoholic' situation I deliberately drink soft drinks so any less confident person can be with me, and not feel they have to drink to be 'grown up' or 'in with the gang'.*

For another Friend, in other circumstances, the need for consistency is paramount:

> *It's a bit like the peace testimony – if no-one did it, no-one would get in trouble with it. If we look with greater vision, it encourages dependency through the gambling industry. I do consider my own behaviour – I ask, 'do I want to be here?' I do want to be consistent.*

A Quaker perspective that Friends in the study often quoted when discussing their own or others conduct in relation to gambling and substance use is contained in George Fox's words to William Penn: 'as long as thou canst.' This phrase comes from a passage in 'Quaker Faith and Practice' in which William Penn asks George

Fox's advice about wearing his sword (a practice at variance with the Quaker stance on peace).

> *George Fox answered, 'I advise thee to wear it as long as thou canst.' Not long after this they met again, when William had no sword, and George said to him, 'William, where is thy sword?' 'Oh!' said he, 'I have taken thy advice; I wore it as long as I could.'*
>
> Quaker Faith and Practice, 19.47

Many Friends referred to these words to illuminate their judgements and feelings in a variety of contexts. Sometimes they were simply useful in recognising the complexities of personal decisions: on many occasions they helped Friends to mitigate judgements of others – or, sometimes, of themselves. For one Friend, these words of Fox's helped in navigating the tension between consistency, example and flexibility within changing circumstances:

> *I do have a struggle with this one, because I do think there is a value in setting an example along with most other Friends – and I can feel very ambivalent about it to be quite honest… I would be most likely to drink with… [fairly close relatives], who might be drinking half a bottle between them with a meal and say 'would I like a glass?' – and I would probably say yes. But I think that a large mixed party, with some vulnerable youngsters, I'd be far more likely to say no. Which is, as I say, inconsistent and hypocritical. I haven't resolved that one… It goes back to the time of George Fox and 'wear your sword as long as you can'.*

This tension was recognised by this Friend, considered within a Quaker framework and held:

*It goes right back to the beginning, that you allow people
to think about these things, rather than saying you should
do this and you shouldn't do that... we do say 'consider',
so having considered, if you've decided what your doing
is O.K. for the reasons that you're doing it, sometimes
perhaps friendship is more important than witness.
Sometimes witness is more important than friendship.
I like the word 'consider'.*

This was also the underlying outlook of a Young Friend, who
described her approach to others as: *'I've made that decision that
I no longer do that, but I'm not telling you that that's right for you'.*
Similarly, an older Friend remarked in relation to alcohol:

*Encouraging something that does harm cannot be in right
ordering... Quaker testimony should be giving guidance –
but I wouldn't dream of saying this is the only right way:
only, do it 'as long as thou canst'.*

Another frequently quoted Quaker value was 'that of God in
everyone' – which had a particular resonance in relation to those
suffering from dependency – again, either the self or others. One
Friend who was able to draw away from a substance problem felt
this process was directly connected with their Quakerism:

*...gradually, after attending Meeting over the years, I
came to believe that if there was 'that of God' in everyone
there must be in **me also** and I wasn't all bad.*

The links that many Friends made between the testimonies and
'as long as thou canst' and 'that of God in everyone' is
encapsulated by one participant, in her comment on the idea of
Quaker 'guidelines':

*They encourage me to form a considered view of the
effects of substance use on myself and others, while not*

being censorious towards others who are different.

The words of Harold Loukes seem very relevant here. He was writing about marriages that end, but his perspective seems to have particular relevance to the testimonies on gambling and moderation – and to the way Friends approach them.

The Quaker view is that...forgiveness is part of God's intention, and that the business of the Church is not to judge but to inspire and sustain...

Quaker Faith and Practice 22.76

CHAPTER 6
GAMBLING AND MODERN SOCIETY

*...testimonies are ways of behaving but are not ethical
rules. They are matters of practice but imply doctrines.
They refer to human society but are about God... A
"testimony"... has a purpose, and that is to get other
people to change, to turn to God.*

John Punshon, quoted in
Quaker Faith and Practice, 20.18.

The National Lottery

Britain Yearly Meeting came out strongly against the National
Lottery, and low levels of Lottery play are revealed in this study.
Many Friends who participated in the research expressed a feeling
of congruence with the testimony and the recent Quaker stance
on the National Lottery. This was both in principle and because
of the way the Lottery is 'sold' – particularly to those who might
be in need of money.

One Friend stated, for example:

> *the whole way that the lottery is marketed is 'your chance
> to win a million'. This really irritates me because very
> few people win a million, and a lot of people spend
> money they can't really afford and don't get anything.*

The traditional Quaker view expressed in the statement about the National Lottery – that it 'fosters the view that it is right to hope for something for nothing' – emerges as a significant one in the study. This view is one of the perspectives that either leads to, or reinforces, a decision not to play, whereas Friends who had played the Lottery often cited a desire to win as a motivation – and found the idea of this kind of gain as less problematic. It is also true, however, that one of the most frequently cited reasons for play was that 'some of the proceeds go to charity.'

An interesting counterpoint on the 'something for nothing' dimension of gambling is advanced by one Friend:

> *Most faiths would agree that one of the highest forms of love is to give without expecting anything in return, which can only happen if people are ready to receive the gift. We usually want the response to our giving to be one of gracious thankfulness or matter-of-fact acceptance, depending on the circumstances, and not guilt and discomfort. Children, people with disabilities, frail elderly people are used to receiving "something for nothing". That may be difficult for them, but we who are in a position to help usually encourage them to feel as comfortable as they can with their situation. Charities too receive our gifts without repaying us except perhaps by giving us a clearer conscience. So if we say that receiving something for nothing is wrong, we put all these people into the wrong, unless we can be more precise about this particular form of getting something for nothing.*[34]

---

[34] *Role Over?*, 4.4

Raffles and 'Draws'

Quakers have traditionally not taken part in raffles, but in the study about two-thirds of Friends said they were prepared to take part in small-scale raffles in aid of charity (though not larger scale ones). One Friend's comment summarises this perspective:

> *I'm fine about raffles – if there's a prize, fair enough. I don't see any harm – I will sell raffle tickets to Friends. Some might disapprove, but I think those raffles do more good than harm. Of course I would respect anyone who decided not to.*

Again, there were also indications that Friends made nuanced decisions in individual circumstances:

> *I do buy raffle tickets sometimes, but sometimes I don't as a witness, and give a donation instead.*

Some Friends also raised the question of free draws and prizes and their similar appeals to greed and 'something for nothing.' Some avoided participating on these grounds – others did so:

> *You've not mentioned 'Lucky Number Draws' by Readers Digest, or some of the bigger health or animal welfare organisations. I'm a sucker for them!*

Friends and modern economic life

While many forms of gambling were not of attraction or interest to most Friends in the study, the connections between gambling, speculation and investment were widely felt to be important, not least because decisions of this nature are difficult to avoid. Edward Dommen has explored some of these issues in an article "We can't help gambling" (*QAADRANT*, issue no. 27). In it, he discusses the many ways in which Friends are 'gambling', including activities central to a modern economy, such as share owning and selling, mortgages, insurance and any risk-taking activity that can be measured in money terms.

Those participating in this study were asked which common activities they felt involved gambling or speculation. About forty-five per cent of the sample considered shares to be a form of gambling; about thirty per cent thought they were not and twenty-five per cent were unsure. ISA's and PEP's were more acceptable: forty-eight per cent thought this was not gambling; twenty-five per cent were not sure and twenty-seven per cent thought they were. Differences of view were not related to age.

As regards shares and investment, there were a variety of views expressed within the study. One respondent's analysis was:

> there should be a difference between buying shares in a company in a long term investment and buying and selling in the hope of making quick gain (or losses). The first reason for buying stocks and shares has nothing to do with gambling. The second is nothing but gambling.

Another feels that 'by investing I am supporting a bit of the economy. It's the way companies raise money: it's related to economic health in society.'

Another: 'Legitimate, ethical businesses need to raise money to create wealth – there's nothing wrong with this.' Another is aware of the dilemma between modern economic life – which necessitates the efficient allocation of capital – and spiritual beliefs. This Friend thinks that Quakers have ducked the debate:

> Investment is about the efficient allocation of capital. Gambling is not about helping an economy to work

*efficiently. Motive and intention are important. It is
difficult, it's all about drawing lines... ethical funds may
have a restriction on what they invest in, but short-term
gain may still occur. Investing is about making a return.
...This debate needs to be had in Quakerism. I'm not
sure that people really understand ethical investing... I
don't know enough about it but its all very akin to the
issues that Islam has with interest, and in the same way
they have to work out how they accommodate modern
economic life with their views and spiritual beliefs... so
it's something that other faiths have had to engage in and
maybe we've ducked to a certain extent.*

The general dilemma is also felt by a younger Friend, who worked
through the contrast between Matthew 6: 26-28 (the passage
about the birds and the lilies and not being anxious about
tomorrow) and other Biblical texts:

*But actually I was persuaded by a completely different bit
in the Bible – that when people have the capability to look
after themselves, they should do so – and therefore create
more capability for those who are unable to. It made me
think that I do earn enough to get a pension and why
should I ask other people to look after me in 50 years
time?*

One Friend in the survey had given these matters particular
thought, and here gives a personal perspective:

Investment and the Society of Friends: a personal perspective

---

Quaker Faith and Practice states that we should resist the desire to acquire possessions or income through unethical investment, speculation, or games of chance. (Quaker Faith and Practice, 1.02.39)

We have seen the rise of Islamic banking in the last few years and many in the Muslim community have actively pursued a debate over financial engagement as a member of the Islamic Faith. As a Society we too need to engage with the issue of investment as it is increasingly part of everyday life and not something that most people can simply ignore.

Ethical investment is something that has become more common in the last few years with many Friends (and also non-Friends) choosing to invest money in a way that fits with their moral outlook and does not trouble their conscience.

There are a number of questions that we need to ask as Friends, though:

- *Can investment itself ever be ethical?*
- *What is an 'ethical' investment?*
- *Is putting money into an 'ethical' fund enough?*

In Quaker Faith and Practice it tells us that we should not engage in any practice from which we receive material gain without equivalent exchange.

This seems to suggest that investment can be ethical as long as one (or someone appointed on one's behalf) spends time under-standing the investments that are being made and actually puts some work into investment decisions – rather than just 'speculating'. This also means that we should consider 'intentions' when considering whether investment can be ethical.

This may lead us to question both our own investment decisions –
for instance, when buying shares in a company, I should be doing
it as a long-term investor who believes in the business and its
objectives – and also those of people we may delegate the
investment decisions to.

Lots of us will be putting money aside in a pension fund. This money
is invested and it is likely that at least a portion will be invested in
company shares; some is also likely to be invested in government
bonds (or debt) which will help to fund that government's
expenditure programme (including defence spending).

We should do as much as we can to make sure that the fund
managers operating on our behalf are making sensible decisions
on our behalf, and invest in companies because the company is a
good long term investment (rather than simply because the
company's shares are 'going up').

So maybe investment can be ethical as long as the appropriate
amount of work is put in to ensure that it is not simply
'speculation'. But what about the area of investment many adults
in Britain will benefit from at some point in life – property?

Clearly if I build my house and then sell it one could argue that
while I have made material gain I have also put in some time and
work. However, the booming house market of the past ten years
has enabled many in society to make a handsome return on the
'investment' that they made in their housing without doing
anything at all.

Is this an acceptable investment? Is it ethical? Some may argue
that they don't look on their accommodation as an investment, and
that therefore the 'return' they have made is incidental. This seems
to reinforce the notion that a person's intentions are critical as to

whether an investment return is 'acceptable' or indeed ethical.

What is an ethical investment?

These are broad considerations, but in a more narrow sense many of us will want to put our pensions with ethical fund managers.

This is a sensible step, but in investing ethically we all need to be aware that a line needs to be drawn somewhere. Clearly definition is important, but investing in tobacco companies, pornography or defence companies are often considered to be unethical. However, what about investing in a bank that lends to a defence company? Or a television station that provides airtime for a pornography channel? Or a newsagent or supermarket that sells tobacco?

We all have to set our own 'line in the sand' over which we will not cross. How strict or flexible we are is up to us, but will play an important role when we come to invest in companies. There is no clear definition of 'Ethical investment" unless we take the strictest.

Is putting money into an ethical fund enough?

First we need to establish why we invest in ethical funds. Do we do it in order that we can sensibly provide for the future while not contradicting our core belief system and morals, or do we do it in order to change behaviour? If the latter, then it is not enough to simply invest in an 'ethical' fund because the company which offers the product may see it as simply another product. By investing in it we are salving our own conscience, but we are not actually encouraging companies to stop 'unethical' investment. Most companies offering an 'ethical' fund will have it as one of a range of products being promoted. The only way to change behaviour in this instance is for so many individuals to invest in

the ethical product that the companies concerned actually sit up,
take notice, and perhaps look at producing more ethical products.
At the very least, when choosing an ethical fund we should make
sure that we are comfortable with other investment funds run by
the firm.

Investment is something that is very much part of society. Some
Friends will try to withdraw from mainstream society as much as
possible so that they don't compromise their beliefs. However, this
is not practical for the majority and therefore we must engage in
a debate over investment rather than ignore it, and the
complications it brings for us as Quakers.

CHAPTER 7

THE QUAKER COMMUNITY

1. Alcohol and the Meeting House

Traditionally Quaker Meeting Houses have been free from alcohol
(and, by extension, from nicotine and any other substances). This
makes manifest the Quaker testimony on substances, and though
there were no questions specifically on this in the study, it became
apparent that this practice had some important wider effects.

Several Friends drew attention to the practice in their comments.
For some, the tradition embodies the benefits of setting an
example:

> *The Meeting House party is a wonderful occasion for fun
> without alcohol. Being aware and in control help me to be
> aware of the spiritual processes within me.*

Another came from a similar perspective, and linked it with the
needs of other users of the Meeting House:

> *In a Quaker context it's acceptable not to drink – I've
> never been persuaded to drink. The premises committee
> had a heated debate about alcohol on the premises, and I
> felt very strongly Alcoholics Anonymous needed an
> alcohol free space.*

For many, the tradition is a representation of the Quaker
community and has a significance that extends beyond Meeting
Houses and gatherings. One Friend summarised it thus:

> *I like being part of a community in which it's acceptable
> not to drink.*

However, Meeting Houses may not be dedicated buildings, or may
be used in a variety of other ways. Some of the issues about
alcohol in the Meeting House were explored in QAAD's magazine
QAADRANT.

Graham Thomas writes in Issue no 34:

When the Quaker Gallery at Westminster Meeting House opened
ten years ago, the Meeting carefully considered whether or not to
allow the provision of alcohol at the Private Views. Three AA
groups were meeting in the building at the time and their views
were also canvassed. They had no objection so long as no alcohol
was left in the kitchen or other parts of the building before or after
the Private Views. This has been the rule and there have never
been any problems associated with the provision of alcohol at
Private Views during the past ten years.

Recently Westminster PM was asked if the Meeting would allow
alcohol to be offered at the reception following the wedding of two
members of the Meeting. There were no objections.

The Meeting House is surrounded by pubs and restaurants, but less
so than in the 19th century, when there was literally a pub on
every corner. Considering the amount of alcohol that must be being
consumed all around us we do represent an oasis of sobriety in the
area – even St Martin-in-the-Fields offers wine with its services!

Ella Kingham Speirs writes in Issue no 34:

A recent discussion at QAAD on the use of alcohol in Meeting Houses made me wonder if our decision not to have alcohol at our Quaker wedding in Liverpool Meeting House was actually more unusual than I thought. It is perhaps worth mentioning that a few doors down the street from the Meeting House is a pub which, we understand, saw a few extra faces that evening! But we were oblivious and certainly no one at the wedding appeared from their behaviour to have been drinking excessively. There were also people popping out periodically for a quick fag and no doubt the odd joint being smoked too, but my sense is that no one saw this as an imposition and totally respected our wish for an intoxicating-substance-free-zone within the building.

From the overwhelmingly positive response we have had, both at the wedding and since, it seems that everyone had a great day and the absence of alcohol did little to mar their enjoyment. I'm certainly grateful that I removed the temptation from under my nose and thus had a wonderful and sober day!

Martin Mottram writes in Issue no 35:

I approve of not allowing alcohol in Meeting Houses, but chiefly because it keeps out organisations whose behaviour interrupts the use of the building for religious purposes. Not by incidental noises etc., but by some sort of spiritual feeling that can be left behind. This can remain for some days. I have also noticed that for me Meeting for Worship is nearly always better in Friends' Meeting Houses than in community halls or people's homes.

I believe that Meeting Houses are places where we can find spiritual growth and warm fellowship without the use of addictive substances... Recently I have found that two of the organisations who regularly use the premises assume the Quakers would not wish them to bring in alcohol and therefore are pleased to abide by this even without being asked.

2. Young Friends' General Meeting

Young Friends' General Meeting is a community that holds many of its Meetings as residential events in Meeting Houses, and issues relating to substances are given explicit consideration. Younger Friends are also of the age where issues relating to substance use are more likely to be experienced and discussed. YFGM members were particularly generous in engaging with the study, and one sense that emerged clearly was the extent to which Young Friends are able to support each other in relation to substance use questions. On a practical level, decisions begin early in an event:

> *...whilst at YFGM we have always tried not to make it seem like on Friday evenings that everyone goes to the pub – provide activities at the Meeting House and stuff so people don't feel pressured.*

This was the general outlook expressed by many. It may not always work for some – though discussion then ensues:

> *You're not allowed alcohol in the building, but you're allowed to bring it back inside you. But at least they're willing to talk it through with me when I speak to them...*

Some Friends now in their late twenties and early thirties also

believed that there had been a gradual change in general attitudes
to substances over the past few years:

> ...there are far fewer smokers [of cannabis] in general
> that there ever were when I was a Young Friend. There
> are far less going to the pub, and its very obvious that
> that's the case. Which is nice... people are happy to be
> with each other as they are...

Nicotine remains a substance of comment for some:

> In Young Friends however I find that a lot of people
> smoke cigarettes and that bothers me and I don't like it.

The smoker may sympathise with this perspective:

> I need it. I would stop smoking if I could; it's not in
> tune with the Quaker event. You do have to go to this area
> to smoke, rightly so...

This consideration about the Meeting House was relevant to the
use of all substances:

> they're on Meeting House premises and that's very much
> not allowed – and people respect that.

One practical and community effect of non-use on Meeting House
premises seems to be the choice to drink or smoke remains
individual (though, of course, a group may decide to go out
together). It means, however, that a decision has to be taken, and
the effects are considered:

> I think in general Young Friends are fairly sensitive,
> there is certainly no pressure, no overt pressure from any
> Young Friends at that gathering or any event I've been at
> to do anything they didn't want to.

Some expressed a sense that there may be a diversity of
behaviour in the private domain, and the potential for an

individual to have an issue with a substance was more overtly
acknowledged than with older Friends. In general, many
expressed the sense that Young Friends is a highly supportive
community, in which personal issues relating to substances could
be raised without fear of judgement or rejection. For example,
one Young Friend who had experienced problems with illicit drugs
and prescribed medicine commented on the help he received from
others at YFGM:

> *When I reduced anti-depressants...and the things that*
> *were coming back into my own mind were wonderful. A*
> *lot of my Young Friends who I've seen come off drugs*
> *have said as well, coming back to yourself is incredible...*
> *I'm not talking here about really heavy drugs*
> *necessarily... I mean I could talk to people – about how*
> *they got on to tobacco, say...*

Another Young Friend commented:

> *I've got very good friends and some of my oldest friends*
> *are Quaker Friends. I always feel I can talk to them*
> *about anything. If I had a problem with substances I*
> *would feel more confident in going to talk to someone at a*
> *Friends Meeting than ringing up a help-line or something*
> *like that.*

As one Young Friend put it:

> *I think Quakerism is very good at that... The whole thing*
> *is about not judging people and accepting them.*

A current member of YFGM gives her general perspective as a
member of the community:

My experience of YFGM: a Young Friend's personal perspective

I hardly drink, have never smoked or taken anything illegal. When YFGM held a session on drugs and alcohol a couple of years ago I was in quite a diverse small group, where some of the group were teetotal and others regularly went to the pub at YFGM. We were able to have an interesting discussion respecting each others' views on the topic.

There are a significant number of smokers at YFGM and as a non-smoker I have not felt any pressure to join in. We usually arrange an area outside where they can smoke and those of us who don't like the smell can easily avoid it.

I have not been affected by other forms of drugs but I feel that YFGM gives Young Friends space to find friends who they can talk to and with whom they feel comfortable discussing anything which is an issue for them. And I feel that in this way YFGM would be supportive of those with concerns about drugs.

We have had some interesting discussions (at meal times) about legalisation, and while there are a range of views, I felt everyone was able to express their feelings on the issue.

3. Residential Events and Friends Under 19

Many Quaker residential events and gatherings involve children and teenagers. Jane Dawson acted as the Under 19 Co-ordinator for the several Yearly Meetings, including the one held at York in 2005. She feels issues relating to substance use are intimately involved with the idea of an inclusive Quaker community – and the issues go beyond the young people themselves. Here she gives a personal perspective.

Organising for an Inclusive Community: Jane Dawson gives a personal perspective

What is an Inclusive Community? One that includes everyone, of course – but unfortunately the answer is not as simple as that.

At Yearly Meetings, as in all our Meetings, we try to be an inclusive community, but who decides what that really means? Do we go far enough to include everyone or does our desire to include everyone act as a turn off which makes some people opt out of the community?

When Friends come to a national event such as a residential Yearly Meeting there are high expectations of what they can contribute and gain from the experience. But do they assume that because we are all Quakers we all have the same expectations?

Take your own Meeting as a model. Is it an inclusive community? Your Meeting House is probably an alcohol and smoke free zone. It should have good mobility access and possibly a loop system for the hard of hearing, but what are the facilities like for the children and do teenagers even enter the Meeting House?

If you were to conjure up a picture of an average teenager, would it be the alcohol sodden, drug affected youth portrayed in the tabloid media? No, of course not. You are a rational adult, but perhaps some of that prejudice rubs off. Maybe you are a tiny bit frightened of teenagers. They so often appear to inhabit a different world from adults; or maybe you have just recollected a moment from your own youth.

Of course young Quakers today are very much part of the wider society and individually may well use a range of drugs, but on the whole they choose not to at residential Quaker events; the popularity of which is growing. York Yearly Meeting is an example of a very large alcohol free Under 19 Programme which, for many, was the highlight of their year. How can we as a Society buck the national trend (or even the reality of your own youth)?

Setting boundaries

Having responsibility for a group of young people there are clearly legal rules which I have to ensure are followed. Any group of young people needs boundaries, some of which are 'non-negotiable' such as those about drugs and alcohol. The groups themselves decide further ones to suit their age. I am responsible for the 'non-negotiable' areas. The group is responsible for policing the boundaries they set for themselves.

Recently I went to a meeting about a school trip for fifteen to eighteen year olds. It was clearly stated that the fifteen-sixteen year olds were not to consume alcohol but the one eighteen year old and staff would be able to drink wine. The Quaker solution might be to make the trip teetotal for all so as not to be divisive and hence create an inclusive community. It certainly would make the boundary issue easier to police and seems common sense in order to prevent the sense of inequality which is often at the root of the rule-breaking

Should we make Yearly Meeting an alcohol-free event for everyone?

Would you want me or any other organiser taking that decision on your behalf? Should it be an issue raised on the agenda of the Yearly Meeting for the Friends present to decide? If we did decide to do this, how many would opt out of our community?

Herein lies the rub. This would be a very unpopular decision and impossible to enforce. After all, for many Friends this is part of their annual holiday; time to relax and socialise and a traditional *bar has a congenial and friendly atmosphere. Friends, many of very good standing, would slope off to the pub and create sub groups and cliques; the very thing we are trying to avoid. So where does that leave our teenagers and what does it say to them? They are being excluded from some of the activities of the community. A group disappearing off to the pub is far more likely to attract the attention of the younger members of our community. There would be little I could do if teenagers, during their free time, (when their parents are responsible for them) decide to have a drink with their friends who are legally allowed. This raises many legal and safety issues for the Yearly Meeting.*

What attracts young people to Quaker gatherings?

Young Quakers today have grown up with the idea of an inclusive community. They feel valued as part of a community for what they are now, not for what they might become. They feel listened to. They know that for a community to function they each have to be aware of the needs of others different from themselves, whatever their age and think carefully about the activities they take part in. For example, if they are legally able to drink or smoke when others in their community are not, to do so would exclude some members of the group.

If we make Yearly Meeting a completely alcohol-free event we exclude some and if we don't, we exclude others. So what is the solution?

How can an inclusive community work?

An inclusive community is a place free from the pressures of the wider society and assumptions about who we are. It is a place where we listen and feel listened to. A place where we are valued for who we are.

When we organise for an inclusive community listening is the most important element and then we throw in a little lateral thinking. We don't assume; we listen to what people want from the event/meeting. No one ever says they want drugs and alcohol; what they say is they want to have fun, be with friends of all ages, to be stimulated, inspired, spiritually refreshed, to feel a part of the whole, to be valued and be shown ways they can play a part in the wonderful adventure called the Yearly Meeting in session. They don't always know how to have all those things and that is our job as organisers.

The first thing to get right is the use of the space. People want a variety of places to socialise, places that serve food and drinks and that are comfortable to relax in. The types of spaces and the range of catering is more important than whether alcohol is served. Everyone wants something different. We have now made our main socialising space non-alcoholic with a range of different catering available. That is the only bar/cafe that is open late. Has your Meeting asked the young people what they would like when offering hospitality and the rooms they meet in?

Secondly, we think about structural changes to the timing of events and worship to make them suitable for all ages, offering a range of different opportunities at different times, suiting owls, larks, those needing afternoon naps. Teenagers want activities late into the evening. If we don't plan for this the teenagers will find something to do at this time. How many Meetings have tried evening epilogues as a way to attract younger Friends?

Like most Quakers, Young Friends don't just want activities put on for them, they want to be actively involved with the planning process. The young people nominate some of their peers to work alongside adults in the planning of the programme. We have had to change the structure of our committees and planning processes to accommodate this. The young people are encouraged to plan and take responsibility for aspects of the programme. They are encouraged to be role models for their peers while being helped to understand the responsibilities and role of the adults. Does your children and young people's committee have any young people on it? Are they given support to take their ideas to fruition?

Most young Quakers have a great wealth of skills to offer and with guidance can not only participate but take responsibility for events. The Hiroshima Witness at Yearly Meeting 2005 was the responsibility of the Under 19 Programme. The ideas came from the young and they were involved from its conception through the stages of risk assessment, stewarding and publicising the event. Has your Meeting lived adventurously and handed over to the young people the responsibility for being elders of a Meeting, organising a witness or running a study group about a topic that interests them?

And what has this got to do with drugs and alcohol?

If you are part of a community and feel valued for who you are now – once respect is given for your ideas, and structures changed to increase your involvement, once you are given the responsibilities of participating in an event – then you don't really need an escape. If all your friends are involved and no one feels left out or needs to prove themselves and you feel listened to, you are unlikely to go out and get drunk and ruin something you have a vested interest in. What greater high is there than getting involved and making a difference?

4. The Quaker Community

The Quaker community does not exist only at formal Gatherings and in Meeting Houses. It has its being in many forms: at Meeting for Worship, certainly, but also within a variety of formal and informal relationships. Anne Hosking reflects on her experience of oversight and eldership to explore some of the ways in which the Quaker community can uphold Friends in dealing with substance use and gambling.

Thoughts on the Quaker community: Anne Hosking gives a personal perspective

---

Culture and context do make such a difference on these matters, positively or negatively. Negatively, people drink or gamble because their friends do, because that is how they communicate and express relationships ('you look a bit low today, tough at the office? Do you want to go out for a drink?'). Our culture embeds these habits in entertainment and sport: think of how the Lottery programme on Saturday evening TV is supposed to be about family togetherness, enjoying an amusing show – or how sporting events and facilities are financed. Positively, what do Quaker Meetings have to offer that counters this, and how does 'it' do it, and is it effective?

Sandra Cronk's pamphlet Gospel Order *offers food for thought on the Quaker sense of community, and the role of mutual accountability.*

> *... those gathered into the church-community have a covenant with God. It is a living relationship of trust, listening and responsiveness to God's call. They also have*

*a covenantal relationship compromising the same
qualities **with each other** (my emphasis).*[35]

*...It [is]admonishing a person to be courageous in
adversity or to undertake a much needed ministry or
service. It [is] encouraging to take a risk in trusting
God's leading or letting go of a behaviour that [is]
blocking deeper commitment to God. In short, it [is]
helping each other move toward greater faithfulness in all
areas of living... We often mature spiritually in small
steps. Awareness usually comes before mature practice.
There is a lag or gap in our lives...*[36]

*...it is obviously necessary for all members of the
community to live in a close relationship of love, trust
and caring.... We cannot love each other into wholeness
unless we know each other well and have that knowledge
anchored in God's love and truth.*[37]

How are these high principles of mutual accountability and
community expressed? In my observation, common examples
would include:

- knowing each other as personal friends, not just as formal
  members of a meeting;

- sociable times together, for example the famous tea at
  Monthly Meeting!;

- activities together, such as joint projects in a local meeting,
  service on committees, working groups, when we have a joint
  calling;

---

[35] Sandra Cronk, *Gospel Order: A Quaker Understanding of the Faithful Quaker Community*, Pendle Hill Pamphlet #297, Pendle Hill Publications, 338 Plush Mill Road, Wallingford, Pennsylvania: 1991, p.22.
[36] Ibid p. 25
[37] Ibid p. 31

- study groups – these so often include shared reflection on our testimonies, on the example and teaching of Jesus, looking at the wider society. When we try to express to each other in words the essence, the deepest values of our lives, we are all challenged, we all grow;

- Meetings for Clearness and similar opportunities for seeking divine guidance in worship – these are not only of great benefit to the person seeking clearness, but are a privilege and a learning experience for the group. The combination of love, honesty and trust can be a source of strength long after the original reason for seeking clearness has faded;

- other opportunities for learning together, for example courses at Woodbrooke on oversight and eldership.

- conferences, representative councils, where exploration of issues in an atmosphere of trust, where business sessions, worship, fellowship all complement each other.

All of these are ways in which the Quaker community shares and teaches its principles, and maintains its ethos. Admonition, example, accountability and a sense of valued identity (all of which are best found in community) go along with satisfying one's deepest yearnings in a way that is creative, working with Divine Creativity. Robert Barclay wrote of 'the secret power' he felt in the Quaker meeting for worship, and how he *'found the evil weakening in [him] and the good raised up.'* (*Quaker Faith and Practice*, 19.21) That to me is what 'salvation' means – not a theological term, but the reality of a good and joyful life in a community of friends.

CHAPTER 8
CONCLUSIONS
by Helena Chambers of QAAD

When I began this study, the purpose was to gain a sense of the experiences and perspectives among Friends in relation to substance use and gambling. As the study progressed, I came increasingly to the view that Friends – acting individually but above all as a religious community – are able to deal with issues relating to substance use and gambling in a balanced way that seems to have some distinctive qualities and some helpful effects. This is not to suggest that Quakers always 'get it right' – as parts of this book attest – and certainly not to deny that other religious groups have their own powerful and distinctive strengths. However, I do believe that Quakerism – that is to say, Quakers and the Quaker community – have some useful perspectives to offer, particularly at a time when the causes of substance and gambling problems are a focus for concern, but the elements of moderate or responsible behaviour receive less attention.

Some ideas and questions from studies of religious denominations were outlined at the beginning of this book. Two proposals derived from such studies were described: the first that a strong standard on gambling and substance use is the best prevention and protection, the other that this may risk excluding some – including those who most need support. My suggestion – based on

the perspectives Friends so generously shared – is that the Quaker
tradition of balance between letter and spirit, anchored and
enacted within the worshipping Quaker community, seems to
enable some reconciliation between these two points.

To put this in terms of the practical results of the study, the
Quakers who took part generally do not gamble and are abstinent
or moderate as regards substance use – but this does not
necessarily mean that all Friends are abstinent or moderate for all
of the time. Some may find the latter point disquieting, but the
ability to hold this tension seems to be one of the particular
strengths of Quakerism – and of Quakers. This final chapter
summarises how I suggest the testimonies on gambling and
moderation operate within the 'greater whole' of the Quaker
religious tradition and enable this balance to work.

The Quaker balance

> ...*the area of imprecision with which they are surrounded
> is the greatest strength of the testimonies. It enables them
> to be flexible as circumstances in the world change, and
> provides individual Friends with a constant challenge to
> work out for themselves what God is asking of them.*
>
> John Punshon, *Testimony and Tradition*, p. 19

On the one hand, Friends hold many of the religious attitudes
associated with abstinence and moderation. In particular, most of
those participating have some ascetic values (including non-
materialism), and this study confirms the idea that these
predispose people away from gambling and substance use. The
Quaker study was unusual in giving particular and separate
attention to spiritual life and it confirms strongly that for most,

spiritual life is generally associated with the choices of Quakers to be abstinent or very moderate. In this sense, the study is significant in suggesting that spiritual life – rather than just religious belief or involvement – is an important factor.

The other important element that is present in Quakerism – and the most influential from the standpoint of previous studies – is that the testimonies on gambling and substances give 'religious standards' that clearly encourage abstinence or moderation. All of these elements play a part in the fact that the Friends in the study are generally abstinent from gambling and moderate or abstinent in their use of substances.

However, on the other hand, the influence of the religious 'standard' does not seem to work in quite the same way as has been suggested for other religious groups – and this is one of the factors that comprises the other half of the Quaker 'balance'. Many previous studies have tended to assume that guidelines on substance use or gambling would have the authoritative status of doctrine, be reinforced by religious leaders and other members, and generally act as patterns for individual conduct. However, as Ben Pink Dandelion[38] has discussed, many Friends tend to be 'non-credal' and non-doctrinal in their approach to matters of belief. The spread of reactions among Friends in the study to the idea of 'guidelines' in relation to the use of substances, with a significant minority having doubts about the idea, indicates that this same approach may be applied to these testimonies.

Similarly, although many Friends in the study regarded the written testimony and advice as expressing standards to be aspired to, Quaker testimony also contains within it the idea of

---

[38] Dandelion, P. (1996) *A Sociological Analysis of the Theology of Quakers: the silent revolution.* Lampeter: Edwin Mellen Press.

personal discernment and responsibility, as John Punshon outlines. This links with the emphasis that Friends in the study placed on the importance of the personal spiritual journey, which may include rough and even dangerous terrain – but 'as long as thou canst' and 'that of God in everyone' are always applicable, both to the self and others. For all these reasons, the emphasis of many Quakers in the study was not just on what people do, but on the process of spiritual, ethical, and practical reflection that they undertake, which is also experienced as being inherently and centrally 'Quaker.' For those who feel they may have a problem with substance use or gambling, or for those who simply feel uncertain or uncomfortable about their inclinations or behaviour at any given time, the study suggests that the reluctance to judge harshly and the inclusivity of the process of reflection can both be vitally important.

Another factor that reinforces this side of the balance comes from the way that Friends tend to approach ethical questions in general. Jackie Leach Scully[39] has discussed this in relation to Quakers and ethical issues in genetics. Her view is that many Friends do not apply general principles to specific situations in a systematic way (in the way that has been implicitly suggested in most previous studies of substance use and gambling). Scully's insight is that Friends tend to mix a series of ethical methods with various values, personal factors and pragmatic considerations – and combine them in a dynamic and flexible process that she calls 'collage'. This seems exactly the right term to describe some of the processes of reflection undertaken about substance use and gambling in this book – and of course explains the difficulties of some Friends in being consistent whilst

---

[39] Scully, J. Leach, *Quaker Approaches to Moral Issues in Genetics.* Lampeter: Edwin Mellen Press (2002).

responding to specific circumstances. This does not mean, of course, that Friends do not operate from principle at all – many in the study did – but that they seem particularly open to engaging in this process of 'collage'.

The general result of the 'Quaker balance' is that the written testimony and advice on substance use and gambling express a perspective that is shared comfortably by the majority of Friends. Though most Friends do not seem to approach them in the spirit of doctrine or prescription, the testimonies – and such practices as alcohol-free Meeting Houses – nevertheless mark a Quaker approach to these subjects. All of this is reflected in the general pattern of behaviour revealed by the study – that Friends tend not to be involved in gambling and are abstinent or moderate in their use of substances. However the many liberal traditions that infuse the letter with the spirit mean that this is not universal, and some range of substance use and gambling behaviours are also present within the Quaker fold.

The effects of the Quaker balance

One of the ideas from previous research is that a strong religious prohibition may result in abstinent or moderate behaviour for many, but result in uncomfortable feelings of 'cognitive dissonance' for the few whose behaviour does not accord with the standard – and perhaps result in such people leaving the group. The 'liberal' part of the Quaker balance seems to have a reducing effect on this kind of feeling.

A similar process could also be the case for some Young Friends. The behaviour of most was of a moderate nature and gambling rates were particularly low. However, some discussed a process of finding a personal position that could include different levels of alcohol consumption at different periods and, for some, use of nicotine and/or cannabis – but this usually arrived at moderation or abstinence over time. A negotiation between personal inclinations and circumstances and Quaker values is often a part of this process. The study suggests that the balance within Quakerism tends to positively reinforce moderation, but also enables Young Friends to retain a strong engagement through the period at which experimentation with substances is most likely. Though it occurred less commonly and in behaviour of a much lighter and much more infrequent nature, there was some indication of a similar process in relation to gambling among a small number of Friends of varying ages.

Similarly, the Quaker balance is also immensely valuable to the small number of Friends of all ages whose higher levels of substance use were related to issues including bereavement, abuse, mental or physical health problems, or emotional disquiet. The ability to work through such painful issues whilst being engaged as a part of the Quaker community was highly valued by these Friends. For some, remaining engaged with Quakerism and Quakers was part of a process that resulted in a lowering of substance use over time. Understanding and supportive attitudes are also deeply appreciated by those Friends who love or care for a person with a dependency problem. The awareness that substance problems – minor or major – could happen to us 'in here' does seem to be particularly helpful and supportive. Though the choice always remains with the individual about how and when to respond, a vital Quaker community offers opportunities over many years, for sharing, support, and progress. Anne Hosking's observations on the practical and 'saving' aspects of community – and the fact that these are common processes for all – seem particularly significant in this connection.

The 'liberal' side of the balance does leave latitude for Friends to make judgements on the basis of purely personal preference or

idiosyncratic interpretation.[40] John Punshon comments on the
kind of selectivity that separates individual features of Quakerism
from the Quaker edifice:

> *I sometimes think that what we have nowadays is more
> like a supermarket. One may wander round the Friendly
> emporium selecting from the shelves whatever nourishment
> one chooses, with very little restriction...*[41]

Indeed, there were a few Friends in the study who said that they
did not agree with the testimony on gambling or substances (a
few who played the National Lottery, for example, did not feel
this activity to be harmful or unethical) – and sometimes Friends
were drawn to gambling or non-moderate substance use for
personal enjoyment or for other reasons. A few expressed the
feeling that the behaviour 'sits outside' Quakerism in their lives.
However, for many of the Friends whose behaviour was not
entirely congruent with the letter of the 'religious standard',
there was a strong sense of personal negotiation with the
testimonies, including in relation to wider Quaker values. While
there might be an element of 'supermarket Quakerism' for some
people for some of the time, this was not a common feeling.
Paradoxically, perhaps, some of the most serious consideration of
testimony occurred amongst Friends whose behaviour departed
from it, as they tested their own inclinations and experience in
relation to it.

The balance found in Quakerism seems to enable Friends as a

---

[40] This relates to wider studies of British religion, which show that people are
tending to accept certain aspects of religious practice and theology but reject
others - rather in the manner of consumers. Grace Davie describes it in this way:
'it is true that religion has become very largely a matter of personal or private
choice.' Davie, G. 1994; 76 *Religion in Britain since 1945*. Oxford: Blackwell
[41] Punshon, J. (1990) *Testimony and Tradition*, p. 23.

community to retain at least some of those who may experience higher levels of these behaviours or be at risk of developing problems. The study did not take place over time so cannot prove this conclusively, but it seems that the relatively low rates of these behaviours in Quakerism are not generally likely to be the result of losing those who do not adhere to the 'religious standard' and leave because they find the inconsistency too difficult to sustain.

As regards those who become Quakers as adults, the strong majority feel a sense of harmony with the testimonies on gambling and substance use: the abstinent and moderate approach of Friends is often part of the 'coming home' feeling. This seems to be at least as true for Young Friends coming to Quakerism as it is for older ones. In terms of the Quaker body, this is significant, because a high proportion of Quakers are not born or brought up as Friends. It seems, then, that Quakers' position and attitudes to gambling and substance use allow Quakerism to attract people whose values are congruent with its testimonies of non-gambling and abstinence or moderation in relation to substance use. However, those coming to Friends and those already involved who behave differently can be retained – and, at best, helped within the Quaker community.

Finally, the study also suggests that maintaining and renewing both elements of the 'Quaker balance' is likely to be helpful in the upbringing of children. A dual emphasis on letter and spirit places these testimonies and their meanings before young people, but also fosters personal responsibility and spiritual growth.

If this interpretation is sound and these effects continue to occur, the 'Quaker balance' described here may be self-sustaining – Friends maintain it by continuing to engage in these processes of spiritual, ethical and personal reflection, supported by an active

Quaker community. We have tried to represent Friends'
experiences faithfully in these pages, and to bring attention to
those aspects of Quakerism that seem to be particularly helpful in
relation to these subjects. We hope that in publishing this book
and in sharing Friends' perspectives on substance use and
gambling in a way that may prompt wider reflection and
discussion within the Religious Society of Friends, QAAD will be
assisting in this continuing process of renewal.

Reflections by Sandra Hobbs, Clerk of QAAD

---

*In the early stages of writing this book, it became clear that
however we tried to divide information and speculation into neat
categories, the words and phrases would continue to move
themselves around like recalcitrant pawns in a Mad Hatter's chess
game. All of us are moving in an endless dance of relationships
both in and outside the Society of Friends, subject to all the winds
that blow through all the fields we walk in and, like the butterfly
quoted in Chaos theory, ourselves capable of starting the breath
that can eventually cause a hurricane.*

*Some of us were born within Quakerism; some came to it later in
life, perhaps from other spiritual belief systems, perhaps none that
could be formally described. The way we regard the use of alcohol,
other drugs and gambling is likely to be just one part of the warp
and weft of each life's pattern. How did we experience their place in
our childhood? If alcohol was an occasional accompaniment to
family life, a glass or two of wine with a special meal, a stroll to a
countrypub on a summer evening, it may not have reached much
prominence in a hierarchy of important beliefs. If alcohol and other
drugs were a major part of life, with all the disruption and
potential for violence and neglect that can entail, then the issues*

could be sharp and painful indeed. If this is the case, there are really only three choices: to use as well, just to kill the pain; to avoid use like the plague it has become; or to try to find a middle-way – and that, with no safe guidelines at home, can be difficult indeed. Even when we leave home we may unconsciously seek the niche that seems familiar. How often do the children of alcoholics find themselves in alcoholic partnerships without even realising the possibility at first? We join groups that socialise as we do, whether that be Bible Class or the nearest bar.

Peer group pressure can be assumed to have relevance only to the young and impressionable – but when we talk about 'setting a good example to others' what is that but (hopefully benevolent) peer group pressure? We are all social animals at heart, craving acceptance from the tribe, and exclusion can seem, indeed can be, unbearable. As we grow older we move into different experiences, different groupings and the experimentations of life can move on to the new realities of finding a job, relationships, bringing up children. All the time we are building on our own experience of using or not using, seeing others use or not use, reading newspapers, seeing films. We are finding what helps and hinders our spiritual lives, making decisions on health grounds, worrying about the future of our children and remembering all too clearly the advices and injunctions we so blithely dismissed from our own parents.

What of our Quaker tribe? We seek, and often find, comfort in the community of our fellow Quakers, people who share so many similarities in outlook whilst often retaining a quite remarkable degree of individuality (even, dare I say it, eccentricity). As our peer groups change, we hopefully gain more confidence within them. We are able to speak more clearly on where we stand, why we choose to be who we are and behave as we do. We have the opportunity to BE an inspiration or influence in all our different *groupings and therein lies the rub. How do we do that with integrity, without hypocrisy, without judging others?*

Many Friends made a point of stressing that our use, of alcohol in particular, would be an example to others – but also made the point that to avoid use in the presence of others if we otherwise might use is hypocritical. One of the challenges we face is perhaps to show by our behaviour that we have a right to choose, and certainly a right to refuse, but that if we choose to use we can do so responsibly and in moderation. The decisions we may face about our possible use of other substances are of course complicated by the legal implications of cannabis use in particular, and the health and social implications of cigarette use in today's society.

Quaker Advices on moderation and abstinence seem to be a source of strength in working towards recovery from dependencies. What the Quaker Testimonies offer to all of us is an opportunity to reflect on the way we choose to live our lives: to consider not only what we do but why we do it. A time to come to our own decisions on where we stand at this time in life, and how we can be reasonably comfortable in the crosswinds of the beliefs and behaviours of others. Neither condoning nor condemning those behaviours, but simply being ourselves and showing it is possible to do that amidst the temptations and distractions of the world around us.

APPENDICES

SOME CONTEMPORARY ISSUES

The social impact of personal actions is a theme woven through
Quaker history and the written testimonies – particularly in
relation to alcohol use. QAAD's tradition is rooted in social
concerns about general levels of misuse and dependency, and
many Quakers in the study included a consideration of such
issues in their own deliberations. We thought it would be helpful
to relate traditional Quaker concerns – and the findings of this
study – to some contemporary issues, so Appendix 1 attempts to
do this. Appendix 2 gives information about the concepts of
misuse and dependency, while Appendix 3 makes connections
between all this information and QAAD's work on public issues.

APPENDIX 1

Does individual consumption or gambling have an effect on the levels of problem use and dependency in society?

The rates of problem use and dependency in a society are the result of an interplay of many personal and social factors, combined with the nature of the drug or gambling activity itself. At the individual level, genetic or biochemical factors play some part, as do life stresses (including social disadvantage) – and some have also suggested that people with certain personal characteristics (such as risk-taking and impulsivity) may be more prone than others to developing problems. Rates and types of problems also vary with the nature of the substance/gambling pursuit – some are associated with higher levels of dependency and problems.[42]

At the broader social level, problem rates are also affected by how readily available the substance is. The fewer opportunities to gain the substance, and the more difficult it is to access, the lower tends to be the rate of problems. In general terms, many studies – most notably in the fields of alcohol and gambling – suggest that

---

[42] Heroin and cocaine, for example are particularly 'reinforcing' drugs with high dependency rates, as is nicotine. In the sphere of gambling, slot machines and internet gambling – which have a short time between staking and result and can be played again immediately – have high rates of problem play.

there is a relationship between general levels of consumption and the level of problems found in a society. That is to say, the higher the levels of general consumption, the more problems arising from consumption there are likely to be.

This evidence led to an idea known as the 'prevention paradox,' which advances the proposal that if individual harm, misuse and dependency are to be reduced, general levels of consumption must also be considered and addressed. This approach to the reduction of harm is known as a 'whole population' policy. It involves treating the community as a whole and implementing some limitations that affect all consumers – rather than specific measures targeted only at problematic users.[43]

To relate this to Quaker perspectives, the sense that we are all part of the same community, and all inter-related, seems to equate with the views of many experts in the field. In this sense, moderation may have a cumulative social impact both in terms of personal consumption that considers social effects, and in terms of a willingness to be subject to measures that affect all consumers equally. Another connection with traditional Quaker concerns is that the greatest impacts of problems with substances and gambling tend to be experienced by less advantaged groups in society.[44]

---

[43] See, for example, Raistrick, D., Hodgson, R., Ritson, B. (1999) *Tackling Alcohol Together* (Free Association Books, London, New York. "There is a strong relationship between per capita alcohol consumption and alcohol-related problems in the community as a whole. Constraining whole population alcohol consumption is central to policy making." (p 104)

[44] On average, men in the lowest social group (class V) consume less alcohol than those in the highest social group (class I). However, the prevalence of dependence increases with lower social class, so the proportion of men identified as problem drinkers is found to be highest in social class V (11%) and lowest in social class I at 6% (figures from Alcohol Concern);'Drug-use is found

Within the Quaker community itself, it is possible to see some links between a 'whole population' approach and Quaker practices (one could relate 'availability' to substance-free Meeting Houses, for example). Connections with Jane Dawson's reflections on the idea of an inclusive community are also interesting to consider.

Does example have an impact?

The evidence on example is associated with that about availability. Social acceptability does have general effects on behaviour as regards both substances and gambling, because people are influenced by the behaviour and attitudes of others – particularly within their own sub-groups. In the legal sphere, social acceptability and cultural attitudes influence both the use and excessive use of alcohol, for example, and they are also significant for illicit substances. This is particularly significant in relation to young people: the 2005 European Report on Drug Use,[45] for example, makes the following comments on cannabis:

Individuals' values and behaviours are influenced by what they perceive to be the normality in their social environment, and this is especially true of young people. If they perceive experimental cannabis use as 'normal ' and socially acceptable (associating it with low levels of risk and easy availability), this may be a key influence on their values and behaviour regarding cannabis use.

among young people from all social classes, yet risky behaviour, such as injecting or smoking heroin, is more often linked with neighbourhoods experiencing multiple disadvantage.' Joseph Rowntree Foundation Report (2000) *Drugs,: dilemmas, choices and the law*; problems are found in greater proportions in those with other dependencies, with mental health difficulties, offenders, and those subject to adverse conditions such as homelessness.
[45]*Annual Report 2005: The State of the Drug Problem in Europe.* European Monitoring Centre for Drugs and Drug Addiction

At a community level, example has an impact in setting a common social norm. At an individual level, personal actions demonstrate exceptions are possible.

Perhaps because of social concerns about alcohol misuse, there has been some recent interest in the general social impact of abstinence. The evidence suggests that the social effects of abstention from a substance or activity are not uniform, but are likely to be related to the general behaviour within a given society at a particular time. Part of the population may be abstinent from alcohol (for example, women in many cultures) but problem use among the drinking population may still be higher than in societies in which a higher percentage of people drink, but cultural traditions are more moderate (Southern Europe, for example). As regards alcohol, some studies from England suggest that the behaviour of the heavy drinking population is more strongly related to that of more moderate drinkers than it is to the numbers of abstainers.[46] However, in some circumstances, abstinence can have a wider social impact.

Abstinence has its most observable effect when it is the social norm, but it can both reflect and affect the general social climate. Prior to the advent of the National Lottery, for example, the majority of people in Britain did not gamble. Many observers suggest that participation rates in the National Lottery made gambling more socially acceptable, so that the subsequent liberalisation in the gambling laws became more possible. However, the level of liberalisation was limited because of the wide social concerns that were expressed.[47]

---

[46] Colhoun, H., Ben-Shlomo, Y., Dong, W., Bost, L. and Marmot, M. (1997). Ecological analysis of collectivity of alcohol consumption in England: importance of average drinker, *British Medical Journal*, 314, 1164-8
[47] See, for example, the oral evidence of Professors Orford and Griffiths and Dr Moran at the Joint Committee on the Draft Gambling Bill, and the evidence of

Perhaps the best-known example of abstinence is the Temperance movement of the nineteenth century, in which Quakers played a prominent role. Contemporary concerns about binge-drinking – and about the less obvious but perhaps more significant rise in other indices of harm – have led to renewed interest in this movement. The Joseph Rowntree Foundation has sponsored research to explore whether temperance could have some lessons or applications to contemporary alcohol policy. Professor Virginia Berridge undertook this work and published her analysis in November 2005.[48]

Virginia Berridge suggests that even before the rise of the temperance movement, drunkenness and excess was already becoming less socially acceptable – but that temperance broadened this viewpoint and allowed it to become more influential, at a cultural and then at a policy level. The movement 'helped change the culture of drinking in the nineteenth century'[49] – alcohol consumption began to fall from the 1870s onwards. This was achieved not just through personal decisions about alcohol use, but through the wide cultural and political involvement of many groups and classes in society. Whereas some of these elements are unlikely to be replicated now, Virginia Berridge suggests that temperance has some useful pointers for the present.

She notes that the movement was not monolithic – and that particularly during the early phase, it included those who practised moderation as well as those who advocated abstinence.

QAAD, the Methodist Church, the Salvation Army and the Evangelical Alliance. (House of Lords 63-II; House of Commons 139-II, London: The Stationery Office.

[48] Berridge, V. (2005) *Temperance: Its history and impact on current and future alcohol policy* JRF Publications. http://www.jrf.org.uk/bookshop/eBooks/1859354203.pdf

[49] Ibid, p. 1.

She proposes that a similar alliance between abstinent and
moderate approaches could be powerful now (departing from the
split between drinkers and non-drinkers). She believes that the
alliance of abstinence and moderation could help to strengthen a
social climate of moderation – for example, through a higher
profile for the fifteen per cent of the population who are abstinent
or nearly so: "'It's OK not to drink" could dovetail with a revised
moderate drinking message,'[50] she suggests. This kind of
approach sits very comfortably with Quaker traditions and with
the perspectives expressed in this study. Virginia Berridge
suggests it would be possible to increase the social impact of
moderation in today's society by those with this outlook joining
together – including across the various faith groups.

Some of Virginia Berridge's other observations resonate strongly
with the experiences of Quakers in the study, including those
related to Friends working through the issues involved in
abstinence and moderation. As the previous chapters
demonstrate, whereas abstinence appears absolute, moderation
can sometimes feel a little more blurred and relative – even
inconsistent. Virginia Berridge, too, notes that "…'moderation' is
much discussed and is the ostensible aim of policy, but what
moderation means is increasingly difficult to define…'[51] She
suggests that more thought about, and a clearer definition of,
moderation would be helpful for individuals and for health
education.

This study provides an interesting perspective on these issues, in
that it brings together the reflections of many Quakers about the
attributes and nature of moderation and abstinence. The

---

[50] Berridge, V. (2005) *Temperance: Its history and impact on current and future
alcohol policy.* JRF Publications, p. 12.
[51] Ibid, p. 12.

recurring themes for Quakers involve personal responsibility, dynamic judgments about the social effects of one's actions, and processes of spiritual reflection. These elements were considered just as deeply as the more literal question of consumption itself. In secular terms, this puts the stress on process rather than on behavioural outcomes or targets. Such an approach can seem woolly or untidy – as indeed sometimes it did to Quakers themselves – but this study suggests that this emphasis actually has some helpful effects (a paradox that not focusing exclusively on outcomes helps outcomes, perhaps!)

This stress on means rather than just ends also has some particular implications when considering the upbringing of children and young people. This Quaker study suggests that the general nurturing of spiritual development and of moral responsibility assist in personal decisions about substance use and gambling. This does not need reaffirming in a Quaker context, perhaps, but these general approaches may represent a Quaker contribution to the consideration and practice of moderation within wider society.

The values shown to be important in the Quaker study – including the awareness that we are part of a greater whole and the sense that problems or dependency can happen to anyone – are also revealed as elements that contribute practically to a moderate and inclusive community. It has been suggested here that the 'Quaker balance' can provide a situation that neither normalizes use (since the onus is always on the individual to make responsible decisions) – nor stigmatizes dependency or those experiencing problems. This balance, too, may have a useful perspective to offer beyond the Religious Society of Friends.

APPENDIX 2

MISUSE, PROBLEM USE
AND DEPENDENCY

There are many problems associated with substances and with gambling, and much debate has taken place about how they can be construed and considered. Problems related simply to intoxication are usually differentiated from wider problems of misuse or abuse. Misuse can be defined in terms of hazardous use (for example, drinking and driving or driving under the influence of another substance) or use that prevents a person fulfilling their normal social obligations at work or at home. In the sphere of gambling, unwise play that results in budgeting problems on a specific occasion might come into this category.

A more extreme or prolonged set of problems are involved in the domain of dependency. Dependency may be physical – in the case of many drugs, increasing doses become necessary to achieve the same effects ('tolerance'), and the substance can then become necessary for normal body functioning. If this occurs, stopping may cause physical symptoms such as shaking, sweating, nausea, and even fits, in extreme cases of alcohol withdrawal. However, dependency may also be psychological. This is often experienced by the individual as a strong need or compulsion to undertake the activity, and a subordination of other areas of life to its continuation – even when this causes severe problems.

As research into addiction/dependency progressed during the latter part of the twentieth century, the psychological and emotional aspects of dependence came into stronger focus, and the physical aspects of dependence such as tolerance and withdrawal were no longer viewed as such heavily defining features. Some researchers proposed that addiction could be considered as a set of learned behaviours, which can be changed by the person if they learn and practise new skills.[52] All this opened up the way to an emphasis on the commonalities between drug addictions and behavioural addictions such as gambling. One such approach, suggested by Professor Jim Orford, described all such behaviours as 'excessive appetites' – that is, 'appetites – desires and inclinations – that have got out of hand and become excessive.'[53]

Jim Orford has suggested the following set of criteria for defining behavioural addiction, and though there may be differences of emphasis between researchers, these broadly represent the general outlook in the study of addiction or dependency:

1. The behaviour is engaged in at an abnormally high frequency and/or volume.

2. The behaviour is highly salient, as indicated by a preoccupation with the object of the activity or the means of acquiring it, feelings of craving for the object that are experienced as irresistible, or experience of distress when the activity is stopped or prevented.

---

[52] See, for example, Heather, N. and Robertson, I. (1997) Problem Drinking (Oxford University Press).
[53] Orford, J. 'Excessive Appetites', *Psychological View of Addiction*, London: Wiley (2001)

3. The experience of the behaviour being out of one's control,
    unsuccessful attempts to control the activity, or behaviour
    aimed at reducing the harmful effects of the behaviour.

4. The subjective experience of mood modification in association
    with the behaviour or use of the behaviour to avoid or reduce
    an unpleasant mood state.

5. The behaviour brings conflict with family members or other
    people, as indicated by lying to others about the activity,
    stealing from others to support the activity, or criticism from
    others about the behaviour.

6. The behaviour is causing harms in other life areas such as
    finances, education or work, physical or mental ill health.[54]

In the field of formal treatment for substance dependence and
gambling, various screening instruments have also been developed.
These give checklists to help assess whether there is a problem,
and of what severity. These are increasingly being used in medical
and advice settings, and those presenting for help may be asked a
set of such questions in order to assist decisions about what kind
of treatment will be offered.

If a problem is indicated by such tests, help of some kind may be
needed to change the behaviour. This could involve elements,
including advice, counselling or skills training and sometimes
medical or residential treatment. Advice centres for various
substances are available in most locations and advice can also be
sought through the GP.

The Fellowships – Alcoholics Anonymous, Narcotics Anonymous,
Gamblers Anonymous and their sister organisations – are all 'self-

---

[54] Orford, J. 'Problem Gambling and Other Behavioural Addictions'. Foresight
Brain Science, *Addiction and Drugs Project*, page 8.

help' groups, consisting of people who are currently experiencing addiction themselves or have done so in the past. They come together to offer mutual support and understanding and to work the 12-step programme of recovery (see also chapter 3). The Fellowships also publish literature that describes addictive behaviour, so that people can decide whether they see common patterns with their own. The groups, available throughout this and many others, are open to all who have a desire to become free of addiction.

Sources of information, advice and help include:

ALCOHOL AND DRUGS

Drinkline: Help and advice line for England and Wales: Telephone 0800 917 8282

Talk to Frank: Advice and information about drugs and services: Telephone: 0800 776600

Know the Score (Scotland): Drug information and advice Help-line 0800 587 5879

Alcohol Focus Scotland: general alcohol advice & help finding services 0141 572 6700

Alcohol Concern: policy, information and training provider. Does not provide advice, but has a useful list of local services on its website: www.alcoholconcern.org.uk

Drugscope: policy and information co-ordinator. Does not provide advice, but has a useful list of local services ww.drugscope.org.uk

Self-help fellowships

Alcoholics Anonymous (AA): Help-line 0845 769 7555
PO Box 1 Stonebow House Stonebow York YO1 7NJ
Website: www.alcoholics-anonymous.org.uk

Narcotics Anonymous: Help-lines: 0845 3733366 and 020 7730
0009 www.ukna.org

Families Anonymous: Help-line: 0845 1200 660
www.famanon.org.uk

Al-Anon: 020 7402 0888 www.al-anonuk.org.uk

Self-help based on skills development (all dependencies)

SMART Recovery (Self-Management And Recovery Training):
Website: www.smartrecovery.org

GAMBLING

Gamcare: charity offering counselling and advice for individuals
and professionals

Helpline: 0845 6000 133 Address 2&3 Baden Place Crosby Row
London SE1 1YW

Gordon House: offers on-line counselling for problem gamblers via
www.gordonhouse.org.uk; also has a residential service. Telephone
01384 241292

Self-help fellowship:

Gamblers Anonymous: Helplines: 020 7384 3040 and (for
Scotland) 08700 50 8881 Website: ww.gamblersanonymous.org.uk

APPENDIX 3

QAAD's work in the public arena

QAAD is always mindful of the fact that we do not represent the Religious Society of Friends generally. However, the pace and direction of some of the social and legal changes relating to substances and gambling have led us to add a Quaker voice to various government processes relating to these subjects.

Within the sphere of legal activities, we feel Quaker values lead to a holistic approach. We have argued for measures that address the 'prevention paradox', particularly those that do not treat people suffering from problems or dependency as a separate or distinct group. In the spheres of both gambling and alcohol we have argued for some 'whole population' measures, being methods that are acceptable to many in society and are effective in reducing the numbers of those suffering from misuse or dependency. We have also felt it important to address the stigma that can still be attached to dependencies, and to point out that no group is immune from problems, including religious groups.

QAAD aims to keep abreast of the evidence regarding illicit substances and tobacco, and to make this available to Quakers, including Young Friends. In workshops with Young Friends we shared information about the environmental consequences of tobacco production and its health and social hazards for workers in the industry. We continue to assess and share the evidence on

cannabis, including recent studies about mental health concerns.
One such study concluded that this is particularly the case for those
with a vulnerability: 'Cannabis use moderately increases the risk of
psychotic symptoms in young people but has a much stronger effect
in those with evidence of predisposition for psychosis.'[55]

In submissions to policy reviews we have argued strongly for a
public health approach to all substances, whether legal or illegal,
and to gambling. Such an approach is based on the health and
welfare of the individual, rather than primarily on crime or
disorder (which, of course, is not to deny the importance of
tackling these problems). Above all, we have pressed for
prevention and treatment measures that address the human cost
of misuse and dependency, both for individuals themselves and for
those close to them. Within this, we have suggested a greater
recognition and incorporation of the spiritual element in
treatment services (for those who express a wish for it). We have
also argued for measures relating to all substances that support
rather than punish the economies in producing countries in the
developing world.

QAAD's discussion papers on gambling, alcohol and other
substances and our submissions to government reviews are
available to any interested Friend who would like to contact
QAAD. We continue to look for the growing points in these fields,
and be alert to the potentials in the work of Virginia Berridge
and others. Our work in the public sphere will be deepened by the
perspectives shared by Friends in this study.

---

[55] van Os, J., Wittchen, H-U., Henquet, C., Krabbendam, L., Spauwen, J.,
Kaplan, C., Lieb, R., Prospective cohort study of cannabis use, predisposition
for psychosis, and psychotic symptoms in young people. Maastricht University,
BMJ 2005: 330 (7481):11.

QAAD briefing papers:

Briefing for Friends on the Licensing Act and the Gambling Act (summer 2005)

Briefing for Friends on the Gambling Bill (autumn 2004)

Summary and comment on *A Safe Bet for Success – Modernising Britain's Gambling Laws: the Government's response to the Gambling Review Report* (Department of Culture, Media and Sport) for QAAD Trustees (April, 2002)

Summary of the Police Federation Report: an independent enquiry into the Misuse of Drugs Act 1971 Drugs and the Law 1999 (chaired by Viscountess Runciman)

Gambling and the National Lottery (September 2001)

Changes in the law relating to cannabis (November 2000)

QAAD Submissions to Government Consultations:

Responses to Gambling Commission consultations about the implementation of the Gambling Act Spring 2006

Response to National Treatment Agency on Models of Care Consultation for Alcohol Misuse July 2005

Briefing Notes on Gambling Bill (October 2004)

Briefing Notes for Second Reading of Gambling Bill (February 2005)

Submission on Drugs Policy to Home Affairs Select Committee (April 2001)

Written evidence on the proposed changes to gambling legislation to the Parliamentary Select Committee of the Department of Culture, Media and Sport, (May 2002)

Submission to Strategy Unit of 10 Downing Street regarding the harms associated with alcohol misuse (January 2003)

Written Evidence to the Joint Committee on the Draft Gambling Bill, 2003